Junior Nkiere Makoloni

Information and communication technologies

Junior Nkiere Makoloni

Information and communication technologies

Third Year of Scientific Humanities

ScienciaScripts

Cover image: www.ingimage.com

This book is a translation from the original published under ISBN 978-620-6-73031-6.

Publisher:
Sciencia Scripts
is a trademark of
Dodo Books Indian Ocean Ltd. and OmniScriptum S.R.L publishing group

120 High Road, East Finchley, London, N2 9ED, United Kingdom
Str. Armeneasca 28/1, office 1, Chisinau MD-2012, Republic of Moldova, Europe
Managing Directors: Ieva Konstantinova, Victoria Ursu
info@omniscriptum.com

Printed at: see last page
ISBN: 978-620-8-87396-7

PREFACE

Today's world is evolving at the pace of computers and the Internet (the information superhighway). All aspects of our society are governed by an organization and administration based on information technology. Computer science, hitherto considered and used as a tool and support for certain national teaching disciplines, must become a real subject of study in its own right. And this teaching can only be done effectively on the basis of a well-written support by a computer specialist, while respecting the country's national curriculum.

In particular, the teaching of this course will lead students to adopt responsible behavior and demonstrate practical life skills in the field of IT.

We would like to thank the Provincial Ministry of Education of Haut-Uélé and the Provincial Inspectorate of Haut-Uélé 2 for their involvement in the implementation of this book, which will serve not only the Province of Haut-Uélé but all schools in our country that organize the Scientific Option.

We recommend that schools fully appreciate the usefulness of IT tools, and that they do more to unravel the mysteries of this new subject, which will turn Congolese children into responsible individuals useful to themselves and to society.

SUMMARY

Computers are omnipresent in our lives. It has become as indispensable as electricity, and there are now very few daily activities in which IT plays no part. IT touches virtually every aspect of everyday life (computers, cell phones, wireless networks, traffic light control, interactions between government and citizens, etc.). It's a sector in perpetual turmoil, with new jobs being created by the thousands.

In his or her own way, an IT learner is preparing to shape the future of the planet. A career in IT means you'll be working to create useful tools for your community. You could, for example, be working to improve the productivity of businesses in your area, or even making major breakthroughs in healthcare or scientific research.

The IT industry needs creative people who can think outside the box to design new solutions. Companies, for their part, are looking for IT specialists who work well in groups and can stimulate each other to achieve convincing results.

But that's not all: IT workers often have the opportunity to make a positive difference in their communities, as their profession is literally at the heart of the great issues of our time. IT solutions, for example, help solve environmental problems, improve healthcare, enhance the quality of education, facilitate communications, and much more.

High school computer training programs are designed to produce graduates with the knowledge and skills needed to work as computer scientists or analysts, and the autonomy to adapt to changing technology. For this reason, in this book we have developed notions of computer networking, database creation and management with Microsoft Access and notions linked to artificial intelligence, along with a few search algorithms.

Table of contents

GENERAL OBJECTIVE

The general aim of this book is to provide third-year humanities students with theoretical and practical notions of computer networks, database management systems and artificial intelligence.

SPECIFIC OBJECTIVES

- Present Ms Access as a DBMS, define the functionalities of a DBMS in general, and apply them to Access;
- Introduce students to manipulating queries to display data from tables;
- Create simple forms from one table/query;
- Create compound forms from two tables/queries;
- Write processing algorithms for the creation, display and saving of data through the form;
- Create simple reports from a table or a query;
- Create compound reports from two tables/queries;
- Print reports and report labels;
- Import other files or databases;
- Export data from databases to other files or databases;
- Securing a database;
- Understand the concepts of simple, thinking or learning robots/computers;
- explain the concepts, characteristics and approaches of artificial, machine or automatic learning;
- create simple flowcharts and algorithms featuring the learning process.

CHAPTER 1: GENERAL INFORMATION ON DATABASES

I.1. PRESENTATION OF THE MS ACCESS INTERFACE

The Access user interface is made up of three main components:

- **The Ribbon** is the strip of tabs at the top of the program window, containing groups of commands.
- **The Backstage view** is the set of commands you see under the File **tab** of the Ribbon.
- **Navigation pane** is the pane on the left-hand side of the Access program window that lets you work with database objects.

Let's remember that these three elements provide the environment in which you create and use databases.

Ribbon

The Ribbon is the main replacement for menus and toolbars. It consists mainly of tabs comprising groups of buttons. So the Ribbon displays main tabs that group together frequently used commands, contextual tabs that appear only when you can use them, and the Quick Access toolbar, a small toolbar that you can customize with your favorite commands.

In the ribbon tabs, some buttons offer a gallery of choices, while others launch a command.

Backstage view

The Backstage view contains commands and information that apply to an entire database, such as **Compact and** Repair, as well as commands that were in the File **menu** in earlier versions, such as **Print.**

Navigation pane

The Navigation pane lets you organize your database objects. It is the main means of opening or modifying the design of a database object.

The navigation pane is organized by categories and groups. You have a choice of organization options, and can also create your own customized organization template in the navigation pane. By default, a new database uses the Object Type category, which includes groups corresponding to the different types of database objects. The Object Type category organizes database objects in the same way as the default database window in earlier versions.

You can collapse the navigation pane and hide it, but you cannot hide it when opening database objects in front of it.

The Backstage view

The Backstage view occupies **the File tab** of the Ribbon and contains numerous commands. The Backstage view also contains other commands that apply to an entire database file. When you open Access but are not opening a database (for example, when you open Access from the Windows Start menu), the Backstage menu is displayed.

In the Backstage view, you can create a new database, open an existing one and perform many file and database maintenance tasks.

I.2. BASIC CONCEPTS

I.2.1. Database

A database is a structured and organized set of data representing a system of information selected in such a way that it can be consulted by users or by programs .[1]

I. 2.2 Database management system(DBMS)

A database management system (DBMS) is the software that enables a computer to store, retrieve, add, delete and modify data.

I.2.3. Types of database

1) Hierarchical database

A hierarchical database uses a ranking order or parent-child relationship to structure data.

[1] https://www.larousse.fr, accessed on 27/11/2024 at 00hl7'

2) Network database

The network database is similar to a hierarchical database, but with a few modifications. The network database connects the child record to various parent records, enabling bidirectional relationships.

3) Object-oriented database

In an object-oriented database, the system stores information in the manner of an object.

4) Relational database

A relational database is table-oriented, where each data bit is linked to all other data bits.

5) Non-relational or NoSQL database

A non- SQL database uses a variety of formats, such as documents, graphs, wide columns, etc., offering excellent flexibility and scalability to a database design.

I.2.4. Main database objects and their roles

A database file contains a set of objects that enable you to exploit the information in your database. Some of these objects concern the entry of data into the database (table, form), while others concern the retrieval of data (query, report).

Tables	Each database table contains data relating to a particular subject, in the form of a data sheet. Example: a Customers table contains the list of addresses of the company's customers, an Items table contains the list of items distributed by the company... This is the fundamental object of the database: any query, form or report is directly or indirectly based on one or more tables.
Queries	Queries are used to interrogate data from one or more tables. They present data in the form of a data sheet, just like tables. Example: a query can quickly select the list of customers from the Customers table who live in Paris.
Forms	This object is used to enter and modify data in a table. Example: a form...

I.2.5. Table creation

Tables are the objects in a database that **contain basic information**. This information can be entered via a **form**, processed via **queries**, or presented in the form of a **report**. As their name suggests, tables are tables with columns (**fields**) and rows (**records**).

A table can be presented in **Create** mode - where you can see its structure - or in **Datasheet** mode, which shows the various records it contains and enables them to be entered.

The table below is presented in Datasheet mode.

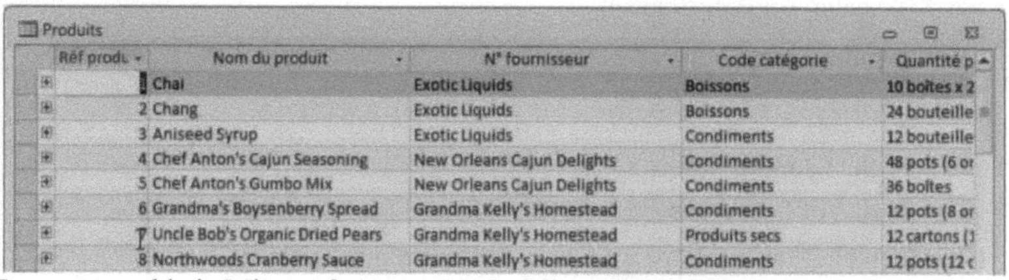

Produits

Réf produ	Nom du produit	N° fournisseur	Code catégorie	Quantité p
	Chai	Exotic Liquids	Boissons	10 boîtes x 2
2	Chang	Exotic Liquids	Boissons	24 bouteille
3	Aniseed Syrup	Exotic Liquids	Condiments	12 bouteille
4	Chef Anton's Cajun Seasoning	New Orleans Cajun Delights	Condiments	48 pots (6 or
5	Chef Anton's Gumbo Mix	New Orleans Cajun Delights	Condiments	36 boîtes
6	Grandma's Boysenberry Spread	Grandma Kelly's Homestead	Condiments	12 pots (8 or
7	Uncle Bob's Organic Dried Pears	Grandma Kelly's Homestead	Produits secs	12 cartons (1
8	Northwoods Cranberry Sauce	Grandma Kelly's Homestead	Condiments	12 pots (12 c

To create a table in Microsoft Access 2010, follow the steps below:

1. From the **Ribbon**, select the **Create** tab.

Microsoft Access 2010 offers two ways to create a table. The Table button lets you quickly create a table structure and enter information. The Create mode also lets you create a field structure and modify field properties. You can always switch to create mode to access these additional options, which are not available in the first table creation mode.

The first part of this exercise will be to create a first version of the **Employees** table using the Table button. You will then need to use create mode to add fields and modify properties.

2. For this exercise, select the **Table** option.

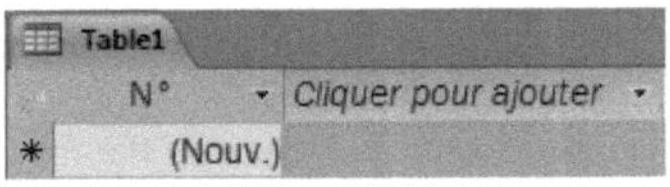	When creating tables, Access always includes a first field of type AutoNumber, which differentiates each record with a unique number that also serves as the primary key. The first step is to change the name of this first field.

3. Place the cursor on the box with the text No ;
4. Press the **right** mouse button;
5. From the pop-up menu that appears, select the **Rename field** option;
6. Enter the name **Employee number**.

Other fields need to be added.

7. Click on the **Click to add** box.
8. From the list of field types, select **Text**.
9. Change the field title, and column title, to **First name**.

You can continue adding fields by using the Click to add button to select a field type. You can also choose a field type from the Add and Remove grouping options.

By selecting the **More fields** option, you'll find a long list of field types with various presentation formats.

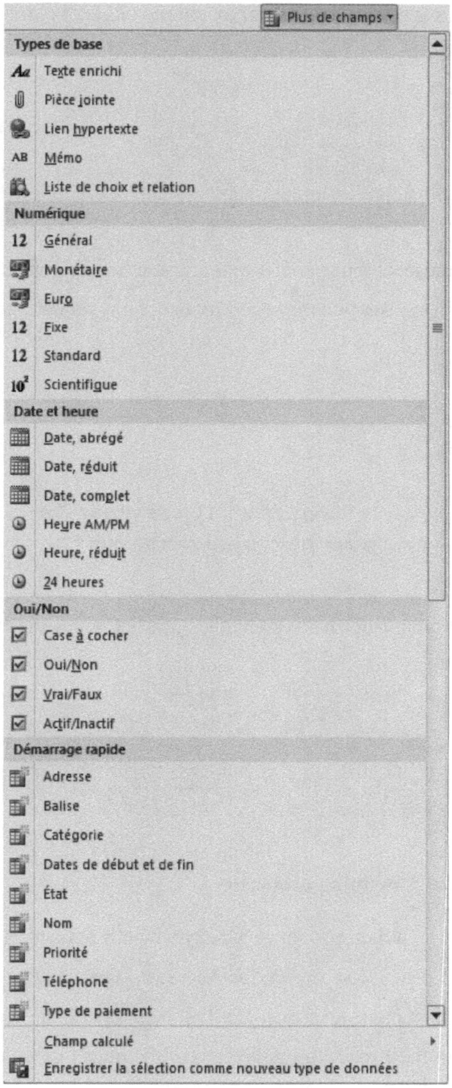

You can also change the field type and some of its properties from the Ribbon options. This is particularly useful for simple tables. Access offers several ways of creating a data table.

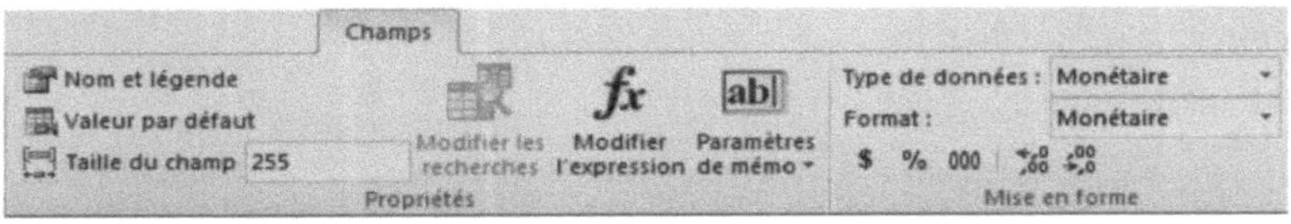

Data sheet mode shows you a grid in which you simply write the information you want to keep. But you may need more options on field properties. To do this, switch to create mode.

10. From the **Ribbon**, press the **Create mode** button.
11. If you haven't already saved the table, give it the name **Employees**.

Creation mode contains all the options for creating and customizing the structure of a data table.

1.2.5.1. defining properties

When you set a property which is defined by Microsoft Access, but which applies to a data access object, the Access database engine does not automatically recognize the property as a valid one. The first time you define the property, you must create it and add it to the **Properties** collection of the object to which it applies. Once the property is in the **Properties** collection, it can be defined in the same way as any other data access property.

If the property is defined for the first time in the user interface, it is automatically added to the **Properties** collection and you can define it as normal.

When writing procedures to set properties defined by Microsoft Access, you should include error handling code to check that the property you are defining already exists in the **Properties** collection.

I.2.6. Relationships between tables

In a relational database, relationships enable you to prevent data redundancy. For example, if you're designing a database that will track information about books, you might have a table called "Titles" that stores information about each book, such as title, publication date and book publisher. You can also store information about the publisher, such as telephone number, address and zip code. If you store all this information in the "Titles" table, the publisher's telephone number is duplicated for each title printed by the publisher.

A better solution is to store the publisher's information only once, in a separate table we'll call "Publishers". You can then place a pointer in the "Titles" table that references an entry in the "Publishers" table.

To ensure that your data remains synchronized, you can apply referential integrity between tables. Referential integrity relationships ensure that information in one table matches information in another. For example, each title in the "Titles" table must be associated with a specific publisher in the "Publishers" table. A title from a publisher that does not exist in the database cannot be added to it.

Logical relationships in a database enable you to efficiently query data and create reports.

Types of table relationships

A relationship works by matching data in columns keys, usually columns (or fields) that have the same name in both tables. In most cases, the relationship connects the primary key, or unique identifier column for each row, of one table to a field in another table. The column in the other table is known as the "foreign key". For example, if you want to track the sales of each book title, you create a relationship between the primary key column (let's call it **title_ID**) in the "Titles" table and a column in the "Sales" table named **title_ID**. The **title_ID** column in the "Sales" table is the foreign key.

There are three types of relationship between tables. The type of relationship created depends on how the associated columns are defined.

One-to-many relationships

A one-to-many relationship is the most common type of relationship. In this type of relationship, a row in table A can correspond to several rows in table B. However, a row in table B can only correspond to one row in table A. For example, the "Publishers" and "Titles" tables have a one-to-many relationship. This means that each publisher publishes many titles. But each title is published by only one publisher.

A one-to-many relationship is created if only one of the associated columns is a primary key or has a unique constraint.

In the Access relationship window, the primary key side of a one-to-many relationship is indicated by the number 1. The foreign key side of a relationship is indicated by an infinity symbol.

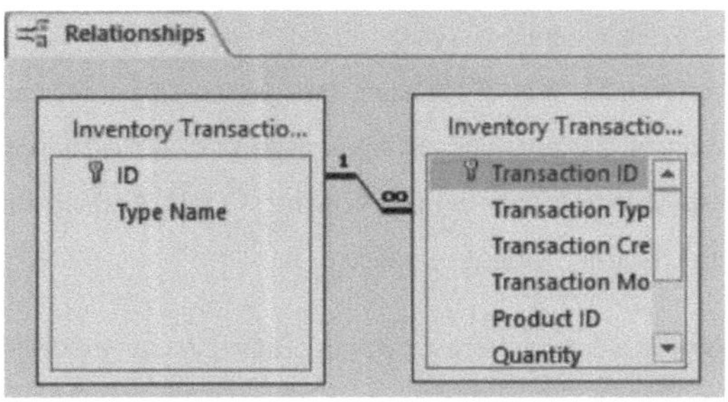

Many-to-many relationships

In a many-to-many relationship, a row in table A can correspond to several rows in table B, and vice versa. Such a relationship is created by defining a third table, called the join table. The primary key of the join table is made up of the foreign keys of table A and table B. For example, the "Authors" table and the "Titles" table have a many-to-many relationship, which is defined by a one-to-many relationship between each of these tables and the "Title-Author" table. The primary key of the "TitleAuthors" table is the combination of the column **ID_au** (the primary key of the "Authors" table) with the column **ID_title** (the primary key of the "Titles" table).

One-to-one relationships

In a one-to-one relationship, a row in table A cannot correspond to more than one row in table B, and vice versa. A one-to-one relationship is created if both associated columns are primary keys or have unique constraints.

This type of relationship is not common, as most of the information associated in this way is found in a single table. You can use a one-to-one relationship to do the following:

- Divide a table with several columns.
- Isolate part of a table for security reasons.
- Store short-term data that can be easily deleted by deleting the table.

- Store information that applies only to a subset of the main table.

In Access, the primary key side of a one-to-one relationship is indicated by a key symbol. The foreign key side is also indicated by a key symbol.

How to define relationships between tables

When you create a relationship between tables, the corresponding fields don't necessarily have to have the same names. However, the corresponding fields must have the same data type, unless the primary key field is an AutoNumber field. You can only match an AutoNumber field with a numeric field if theFieldSizeproperty parameter is the same for both matching fields. For example, you can match an AutoNumber field with a numeric field if theFieldSizeproperty of both fields is a long integer. Even when the two corresponding fields are numeric fields, the sameFieldSizeproperty value must be the same.

How to define a one-to-many or one-to-one relationship

To create a one-to-many or one-to-one relationship, proceed as follows:

1. Close all tables. You cannot create or modify relationships between open tables.
2. In Access 2002 and Access 2003, proceed as follows:
    1. Press F11 to switch to the Database window.
    2. In the **Tools** menu, click on **Relations**.

    In Access 2007, Access 2010 or Access 2013, click on **Relations** in the **Show/Hide** group under the **Database Tools** tab.

3. If you haven't yet defined any relationships in your database, the **Show Table** dialog box appears automatically. If you wish to add tables to be linked, but the **Show Table** dialog box does not appear, click on **Show Table** in the **Relationships** menu.
4. Double-click on the names of the tables you wish to link, then close the **Show Table** dialog box. To create a relationship between a table and itself, add the table twice.
5. Drag the field to be linked from one table to the corresponding field in the other. To drag multiple fields, press Ctrl, click on each field and drag.

    In most cases, you'll need to drag the primary key field (shown in bold) from one table to a similar field (often with the same name) called the foreign key in the other table.

6. The **Modify relationships** dialog box appears. Make sure that the field names displayed in both columns are correct. You can modify the names if necessary.

    Set relationship options if necessary. If you need information on a specific item in the **Modify relationships** dialog box, click on the question mark button, then on the item in question. (These options will be explained in depth later in this article).

7. Click on **Create** to create the relationship.
8. Repeat steps 4 to 7 for each pair of tables to be linked.

   When you close the **Modify relationships** dialog box, Access asks if you wish to save the layout. Whether or not you save the layout, the relationships you create are saved in the database.

Defining a many-to-many relationship

To create a many-to-many relationship, proceed as follows:

1. Create the two tables that will have a many-to-many relationship.
2. Create a third table. This is the join table. In the junction table, add new fields that have the same definitions as the primary key fields in each table you created in step 1. In the join table, primary key fields function as foreign keys. You can add other fields to the join table, as with any other table.
3. In the join table, define the primary key to include the primary key fields of the other two tables. For example, in a "TitleAuthor" join table, the primary key is made up of the **OrderID** and **ProductID** fields.

NB: To create a primary key, proceed as follows:

1. Open a table in create mode.
2. Select the field(s) you wish to define as the primary key. To select a field, click on the row selector of the desired field. To select multiple fields, hold down the Ctrl key and click on the row selector for each field.
3. In Access 2002 or Access 2003, click on **Primary Key** in the toolbar.

In Access 2007, click on **Primary Key** in the **Tools** group under the **Creation** tab.

NB: If you want the order of the fields in a multi-field primary key to be different from the order of the fields in the table, click on Index in the toolbar to display the Index dialog box, then rearrange the field names in the index named PrimaryKey.

4. Define a one-to-many relationship between each primary table and the joining table.

CHAPTER 2: QUERIES

11.1. DEFINITION

A database query allows you to use commands to ask a specific data-related question based on a predefined code. A database management system (DBMS) is created to define a query, the system then searches for an answer directly in the database before extracting and displaying it.

11.2. DIFFERENT TYPES OF QUERIES

Queries are used to display only certain data contained in tables, according to certain criteria.

They can also be used to modify existing tables or create new ones.

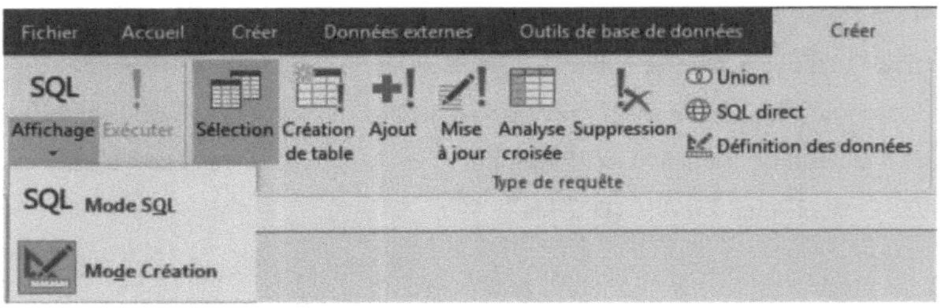

The buttons below are accessible from the Query Tools that appear when you edit a query.

	**selection query**	The Selection query is the most common type of query. It retrieves data from one or more tables, according to one or more selection criteria, and displays the results in the form of a data sheet.
	**table creation query**	Creates a new table based wholly or partially on data from other tables.
	**update query**	Makes global changes to a group of records in one or more tables. For example, increase the price of an item category by 3%.
	add request	Adds a group of records from one or more tables to the

		end of another table.
	**delete query**	Permanently deletes a group of records from one or more tables.

Some buttons

	The **Execute** button allows you to obtain the results of a query in the form of a data sheet before saving it.
	The **Show Table** button lets you add an additional table to an existing query.
	The **Totals** button displays a line of operations (sum, average, standard deviation, etc.) in the query editing grid.

II.3. DIFFERENT QUERY CREATION MODES

A. In Create mode

When you use Create mode to add data sources, you add data sources and fields in separate steps. However, you can always add more data sources later if you wish.

1. On the **Create** tab, in the **Queries** group, click on **Query creation**.

2. Double-click on each data source you wish to use or select each data source, then click on **Add**.

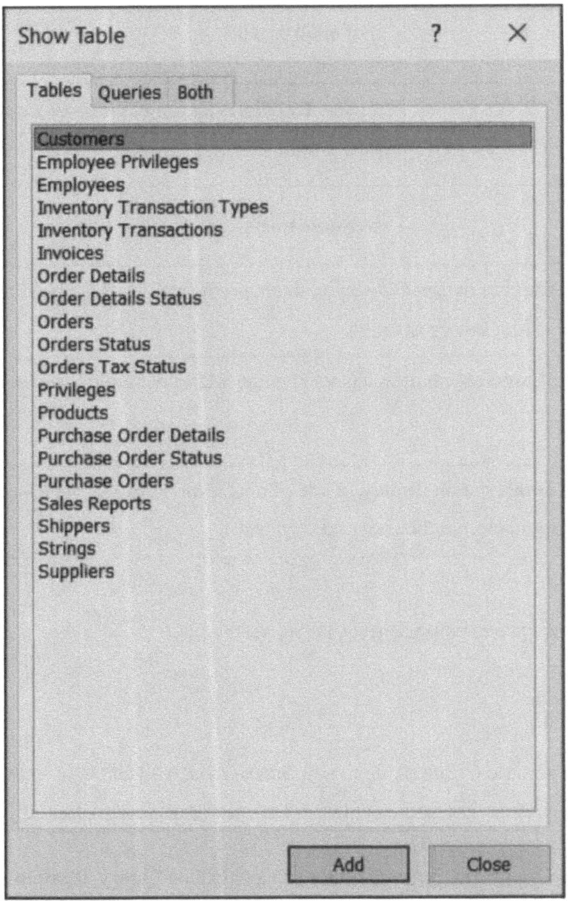

Automatic joins

When you add data sources, if the sources already have relationships defined between them, these are automatically added to the query in the form of joins. Joins specify how data from related sources are combined. Access automatically creates a join between two tables if their fields have compatible data types and one field corresponds to a primary key.

You may wish to adjust the joins created by Access. Access determines the type of join to create based on the relationship represented by the join. If Access creates a join, but there is no defined relationship, Access creates an internal join.

If Access automatically creates the correct joins when you add the data sources, you can proceed to step 3: add destination fields.

Using the same data source several times

In some cases, you may wish to join two copies of the same table or query, known as a reflexive join, which combines records from the same table when matching values exist in the joined fields. For example, suppose you have an Employees table in which the ReportsTo field for each employee's record displays the manager's ID instead of the name. You can use an auto-join to display the manager's name in each employee's record instead.

When you add a data source a second time, Access adds _1 to the name of the second instance. For example, if you add the Employees table twice, the second instance would be named Employees_1.

Step 2: Join related data sources

If the data sources you add to a query already have relationships, Access automatically creates an internal join for each relationship. If referential integrity is applied, Access also displays a "1" above the join line to indicate which table is on the "one" side of a one-to-many relationship, and the infinity symbol (∞) to indicate which table is on the "many" side.

If you add queries to your query and have not created relationships between them, Access does not automatically create joins between these queries, or between queries and tables that are not related. If Access doesn't create joins when you add data sources, you'll usually have to add them yourself. Data sources that are not linked to another data source can cause problems with query results.

You can also change the type of a join (inner join to outer join) so that your query includes more records.

Add a join

- To add a join, drag a field from one data source to a corresponding field in another data source.

Access displays a line between the two fields to indicate that a join has been created.

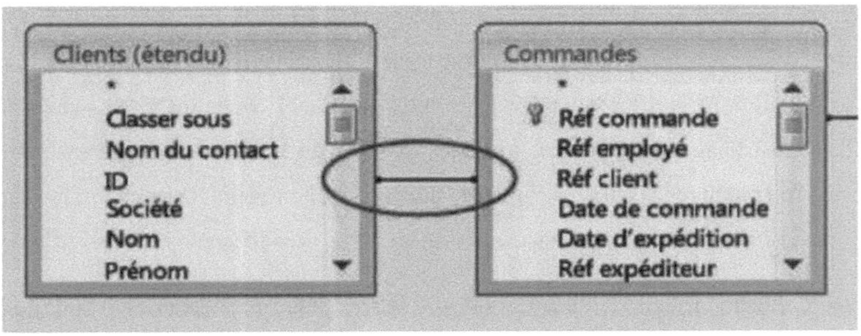

Modify a join

1. Double-click on the join you wish to modify.

The Joint Properties dialog box appears.

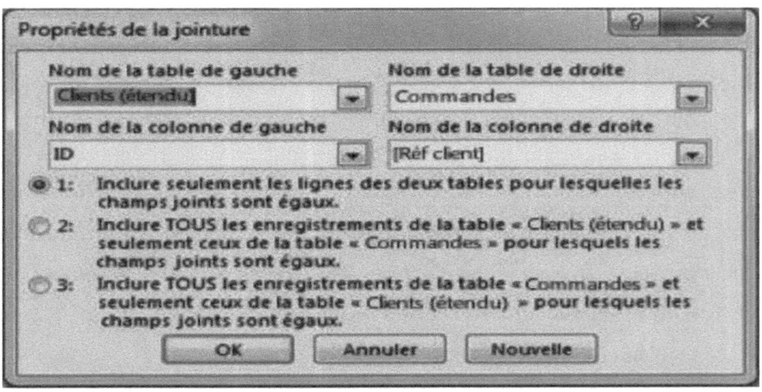

2. In the **Joint Properties** dialog box, review the three options.
3. Click on the option you wish to use, then on **OK**.

Once the joins are ready, you add destination fields (fields that include the desired data in the query results).

Step 3: Add destination fields

You can easily add a field from the data sources you added in step 1.

- To add a field, drag it from a data source into the top pane of the upper pane of the query creation window to the **Field** line in the creation grid, in the lower pane of the query creation window.

When you add a field in this way, Access automatically populates the **Table** line of the creation grid to reflect the field's data source.

Tip: If you want to quickly add all fields to the Field row of the query creation grid, double-click on the table or query name in the upper pane to select all fields from this source, then drag them all to the creation grid at the same time.

Use an expression as a destination field

If you want to perform calculations or use a function to generate the query result, you can use an expression as the destination field. An expression can use data from a query data source, as well as functions such as Format or InString, and can also contain constants and arithmetic operators.

1. In an empty column of the query creation grid, right-click on the **Field** line, then click on **Zoom** in the context menu.
2. In the **Zoom** area, type or paste your expression. Precede your expression with the name you want to use for the result of the expression, followed by a colon. For example, if you want to name the expression "Last update", you'd start your expression with **Last update:**.

Note: Expressions can be used to perform a variety of operations. A detailed explanation of expressions is beyond the scope of this article.

Step 4: Specify criteria

This step is optional.

Criteria allow you to limit the records returned by your query, depending on whether the field values match the criteria you specify.

Specify criteria for a destination field

1. In the query creation grid, in the **Criteria** line of the field containing the values you want to limit, type an expression that the field values must satisfy to be included in your results. For example, if you want to limit a query so that only records for which the City field value is Orleans, type **Orleans** in the **Criteria** line below this field.
2. You can specify other criteria in the **Or** line below the **Criteria** line.

If you specify other criteria, a field value can match the listed criteria and be included in the query results.

Multiple field criteria

You can use criteria with multiple fields. In this case, all criteria in a given **Criteria** or **Or** row must be checked for the record to be included.

Specify criteria using a field you don't want to use as a result

You can add a field to your query design and not include the field data in the query result. You can do this if you want to use the field's values to limit the query results, but not display them.

1. Add the field to the creation grid.
2. Deactivate the checkbox in the **Show** field line.
3. Specify the criteria as you would for a destination field.

Step 5: Summarize data

This step is optional.

You can summarize data, particularly if it's numerical. For example, you may want to determine the average price or total sales.

To summarize data in a query, you can use the **Total** line. By default, the **Total** line does not appear in Create mode.

1. Once the query is open in **Create** mode, in the **Query Creation** tab, in the **Show/Hide** group, click on **Totals.**

   Access displays the **Total** line in the query creation grid.

2. For each field you want to summarize, select the function to be used from the list in the **Total** line. The functions available depend on the field's data type.

Step 6: Display results

To display the results of your query, click on **Execute** in the **Query creation** tab. Access displays the results of your query in Datasheet mode.

To make further changes to the query, click on **Home> View> Design mode** to return to Design mode.

Modify your fields, expressions or criteria and run the query again until it returns the desired data.

11.4. DISPLAYING QUERIES

To display query results, click on **Execute** in the **Query Creation** tab. Access displays the results of your query in Datasheet mode.
To make further modifications to the query, click on **Home> View> Design mode** to return to Design mode.
Modify your fields, expressions or criteria and run the query again until it returns the desired data.

11.5. THE IMPORTANCE OF QUERIES THE TARGET PROCESSING OF DATABASE DATA

Using a query makes it easier to display, add, delete or modify data in your Access database. Here are some other reasons to use queries:

- Quickly find specific data by filtering on specific criteria (conditions)
- Calculate or synthesize data

- Automate data management tasks, such as periodically reviewing the most up-to-date data.

CHAPTER 3: FORMS

111.1. CONCEPT DEFINITIONS

111.1.1. Input mask form

Input masks are a way of restricting the data users enter in form fields, and imposing specific formatting. They are suitable for data such as telephone and credit card numbers, dates and much more.

For example, if you ask for a zip code, you can ensure that people can only submit correctly formatted data - if the format is correct.

111.1.2. Subforms

A sub-form is a form inserted into another form. The basic form is called the main form, while the form included in the main form is called a sub-form.

111.1.3. Header

Headers are the zones that appear in the body and footer of **each form.**

111.1.4. Form body and footer

The body and footer of a form are zones positioned respectively inside and at the bottom of each page of a form. They can be continuous from one section to the next.

III.2. DIFFERENT WAYS OF CREATING FORMS

III.2.1. Create a form with the Form tool

Create a form with a single click, using the Form tool. When you use this tool, all the fields of the underlying data source are placed in the form. You can start using the new form immediately, or modify it in Page or Design mode to suit your needs.

Use the Form tool to create a form

1. In the navigation pane, click on the table or query containing the data you wish to include in the form.
2. In the Creation tab, in the Forms group, click on Form.

Access creates the form and displays it in Layout mode. This mode allows you to make changes to the structure of the form while the data is still displayed. For example, you can adjust the size of text boxes to suit the data to be displayed, if required.

If Access finds a single table that has a one-to-many relationship with the table or query you've used to create the form, Access adds a data sheet to the form based on the associated table or query. For example, if you create a simple form based on the Employees table, and a one-to-many relationship is already defined between the Employees table and the Orders table, the data sheet displays all the records in the Orders table related to the current Employee record. If you don't need the data sheet, you can delete it from the form. If there are several tables with a one-to-many relationship with the table you used to create the form, Access does not add data sheets to the form.

III.2.2.Creating a double-view form using the Double View Form tool

A double-view form offers two simultaneous views of data: form mode and data sheet mode.
A double-view form is different from a form/sub-form combination in that both views are attached to the same data source and are always synchronized. So, if you select a field in one part of the form, the same field is selected in the other part of the form. You can add, modify or delete data in either part of the form (provided the record source is editable and you haven't configured the form to prevent these operations).

The use of dual-view forms allows you to benefit from the advantages of these two types of form within a single form. For example, you can use the Datasheet part of the form to quickly find a record, and then use the Form part to display or modify the record.

To create a double-view form using the Double View Form tool :

1. In the navigation pane, click on the table or query containing the data you wish to include in the form. Alternatively, open the table or query in Datasheet mode.
2. In the Create tab, in the Forms group, click on More forms, then on Double view form.

Access creates the form and displays it in Layout mode. This mode allows you to make changes to the structure of the form while the data is still displayed. For example, you can adjust the size of text boxes to suit the data to be displayed, if required.

III.2.3. Creating a form displaying multiple records using the Multiple Elements tool

When you create a form using the Form tool, the form created by Access displays a single record at a time. If you want to create a form that displays multiple records, but is more customizable than a data sheet, you can use the Multiple Elements tool.

1. In the navigation pane, click on the table or query containing the data you wish to include in the form.
2. On the Create tab, in the Forms group, click on More forms, then on Multiple elements.

Access creates the form and displays it in Layout mode. In this mode, you can modify the structure of the form while the data is still displayed.

When you use the Multiple Elements tool, the form created by Access resembles a data sheet. Data is arranged in rows and columns, and you see several records at a time. However, a multi-element form offers more customization options than a data sheet, allowing you to add graphical elements, buttons and other controls.

111.2.4. Creating a form with PAssistant Form

To better select the fields to be displayed in your form, you can use the Form Wizard rather than the various form creation tools mentioned above. You can also specify the way in which data is grouped and sorted, and use fields from several tables or queries, provided you have previously defined the relationships between tables and queries.

1. On the Design tab, in the Forms group, click on Form Wizard.
2. Follow the instructions provided on the Form Wizard pages.

   Note: If you wish to include fields from several tables or queries in your form, do not click Next or Finish after selecting the fields for the first table or query on the first page of the Form Wizard. Instead, repeat the steps to select a table or query, then click on the additional fields you wish to include in the form. Click **Next** or **Finish** to continue.

3. On the last page of the Wizard, click on **Finish**.

111.2.5. Creating a form using the Blank Form tool

If the Wizard or the form creation tools don't meet your needs, you can use the Blank Form tool to create a form. This tool will enable you to create a form very quickly, especially if you're planning to place only a few fields on it.

1. In the **Creation** tab, in the **Forms** group, click on **Blank form**.

   Access opens an empty form in Layout mode and displays the Field **List** pane.

2. In the **Field List** pane, click on the plus sign (+) next to the table(s) containing the fields you wish to include in the form.
3. To add a field to the form, double-click on it or drag it onto the form.
   - After adding the first field, you can add several fields at once by holding down the CTRL key, clicking on several fields and simultaneously dragging them to the form.
   - The order of the tables listed in the **Field List** pane may vary, depending on the part of the form selected. If the field you wish to add is not visible, try selecting another part of the form and adding the field again.
4. Use the tools in the **Header/Footer** group on **the Create** Form **Layout** tab to add a logo, title or date and time to the form.
5. Use the tools in the **Controls** group of the Form Layout **Creation** tab to add a wider variety of controls to the form.

   To select more controls, switch to Design mode by right-clicking on the form, then clicking **Design mode**.

III.3. DIFFERENT DISPLAY MODES

As you have already learned from some of the articles mentioned in the previous sections, Access forms can be viewed in three different views (Form mode, Create mode and Page mode). It can be useful to know which view to use for a specific task. For example, you can use either Create or Page mode to customize a form. Form mode is the default view for a form. It is mainly used to display a form with data, or to enter data. As the Layout and Design views are used to make modifications to a form, consult the resources in the following table for more information on using these views.

Display type	Used for
Page mode	Make most modifications to a form. You can see the data as you modify the design, which is very useful when setting the size of controls or any other design modification that affects the appearance and user-friendliness of the form.
Design mode	make changes that require a more detailed display of the form structure, such as the Header, Details and Footer sections; you can't see the underlying data when making changes.in Create mode. What's great about Create mode? • Ability to add a wider variety of controls, such as linked object frames, page breaks and graphics. • Modify text zone control sources without using the property sheet. • Resize form sections. Modify certain form properties that cannot be modified in Page mode

III.4. PARTS OF A FORM

III.4.1.Table

Tables are essential objects in a database, as they store all information or data. For example, a company database might contain a Contacts table, which stores suppliers' names, e-mail addresses and telephone numbers. Since other database objects are heavily dependent on tables, you should always start the design of a database by creating all its tables, followed by the other objects. Before creating tables in Access, consider your needs and determine all the tables you may require

A relational database like Access generally comprises several linked tables. In a well-designed database, each table stores data on a specific subject, such as employees or products. A table contains records (rows) and fields (columns). Fields have different data types, such as text, numbers, dates and hyperlinks.

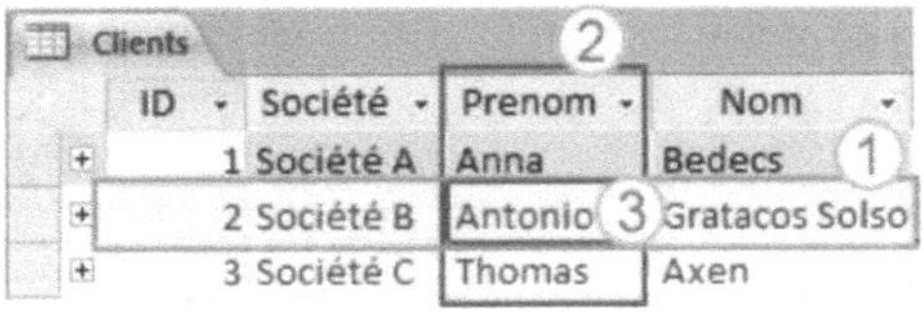

1. A record: contains specific data, such as information on a specific employee or product.
2. A field: contains data concerning one aspect of the table subject, for example first name or e-mail address.
3. A field value: each record has a field value. For example, Contoso, Ltd. or .xyz@example.com

Table and field properties

Tables and fields also have properties that you can define to control their characteristics or behavior.

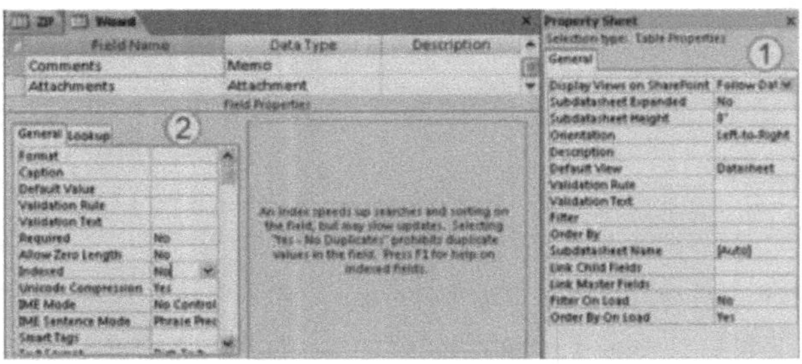

1. Table properties
2. Field properties

In an Access database, table properties are attributes that affect the appearance or behavior of the table as a whole. Table properties are defined in the table's property sheet, in Create mode. For example, you can set a table's **Default Display** property to specify how the table is displayed by default.

A field property applies to a specific field in a table, and defines one of the characteristics or aspects of the field's behavior. You can define certain field properties in Datasheet mode. You can also define any field property in Create mode using the </c0>Field Properties</c0> pane.

III.4.2.Query

In a well-designed database, the data you want to present via a form or report is usually found in several tables. A query can extract information from different tables and assemble it for display in the form or report. A query can be a request for data results from your database or an action on the data, or both. A query can give you an answer to a simple question, perform calculations, combine data from different tables, add, modify or delete data from a database. Because queries are so versatile, there are many different types, and you can create a query type based on the task.

Main query types	**Use**
Select	To retrieve data from a table or perform calculations.
Action	Add, modify or delete data. Each task has a specific Action query type.

III.5. OBJECT TYPES

Access is made up of several distinct objects: TABLES, QUERIES, FORMS, STATEMENTS, MACROS and MODULES. When you use Word, you produce a single file type: Documents: Whether invoices, novels or flyers, you always use the same thing: you start with an empty document and transform it. With Excel, it's the same: you use and produce just one type of file: spreadsheets.

Access, on the other hand, is made up of several objects, as follows:

Tables	Tables are the basic Access object. They're a kind of spreadsheet, to use Excel's vocabulary. With Excel, you have an .XLS file containing several tabs. With Access, you'll have a .MDB database file containing several tables: it's very similar. In the tables, you can store customers, suppliers, invoicing data, membership lists, etc... Tables are used to **STORE** data.

Queries	Queries are filters. With Excel, when you want to sort data or extract a part of it, you have to manage with the menu Data/Sort, or Data/Filter/Automatic filter: If you're a bit used to Excel, you should see what I mean. You always have to be careful not to mix or truncate data by mistake. With Access, we actually have an object: the query, which enables us to save the various filters: for example, you could have a query that memorizes all customers who are over 1M80 tall, who wear a hat and a moustache, or customers who were born in Paris in the 60s, sorted alphabetically by first name, and so on. Queries are also used to perform calculations. For example, if you have employees in a table, and in a column you have indicated their gross salary, you can use a query to automatically calculate their net salary, for example. Queries are therefore used to **SORT, FILTER and CALCULATE** data stored in tables.
Forms	Forms are graphical interfaces. When you go on vacation, you're usually a little reluctant to let anyone rummage around in your Excel spreadsheets: misfortune happens so quickly! How are you going to find your precious files when you get back? Access provides forms: in other words, you'll be able to build masks for entering and modifying data reliably and easily, so that even those who don't know much about computers can still enter or search for data (the mechanism for simply entering data into a database is called an "Entry Operator"). If you go to the Tools/Options menu (in Access, not in Internet Explorer), you'll see that you can change Access' general operating options, but that's not really what I wanted to illustrate, what I wanted to say is that you've got it easy: You can't go wrong: Drop-down lists, checkboxes, boxes, titles: Everything is there to make your choices and your "entry" of options easier:

<table>
<tr><td></td><td>
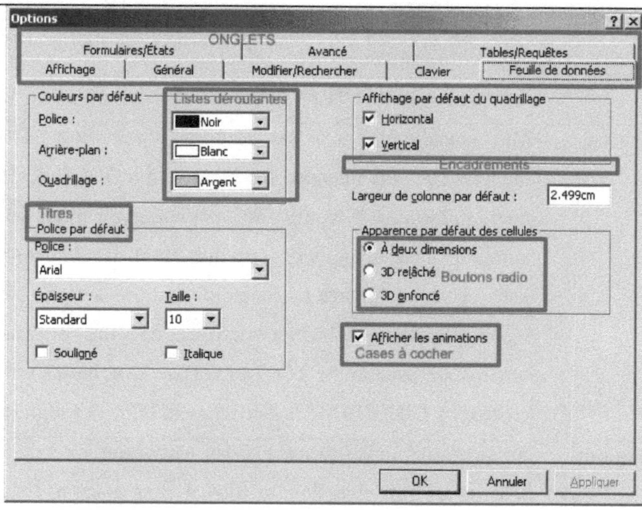

Well, the form is a bit like that: It's about creating a user-friendly environment: You design the form, but it may be other people who enter the data.
Forms are a user-friendly way of ENTERING and MODIFYING data stored in tables.
</td></tr>
<tr><td>Reports</td><td>
Reports are printouts of data. In Word or Excel, you go to the print preview, and you can set two or three parameters: page headers, enlargement or reduction, number of copies required, etc.
Access will enable you to create absolutely impeccable layouts: you'll be able to represent the same data in several different ways. That's right: with Excel, you define the print preview once and for all.... If you suddenly want to change the look of the printout (for example, by printing with the sheet horizontally), you're all set to change the print preview... One spreadsheet = ONE print preview (although that's not quite true)!
Access will even give different names to your printouts. For example, let's imagine you have a list of customers in one of your tables: you could have a report called "List of customers in 3 columns", another report based on the same data called "List of customers with full address", and yet another
</td></tr>
</table>

	called "List of customers over six feet tall, sorted alphabetically"... The number of print previews is infinite. Reports are used to **PRINT** data.
Macros	Macros and modules are not such important objects: These macros and modules are only intended for users with a GOOD command of tables, queries, forms and reports. For example, you might have a command button on a customer entry form that automatically calls up a "Customer list" report: you'll have to design this button yourself, and to call up this report, you'll have to build a macro that does this for you. Macros are used to **AUTOMATIZE** actions, but can only be used and created by **CONFIRMED** Access users (You in a number of lessons).
Modules	Modules are similar to macros, but are written directly in Visual Basic. Macros are still accessible to good Access users, as they are "relatively easy" to use. Modules, on the other hand, are definitely not for the general public. You'll build your first module when you've spent many long hours designing several different databases, and you feel you're about to become a database designer. Only a tiny percentage of Access users and designers master modules. Modules are used to **AUTOMATIZE** actions, but in ways a thousand times more complex and sophisticated than macros.

III.6. FIELDS

Every Access table is made up of fields. The properties of a field describe the characteristics and behavior of the data added to this field. A field's data type is the most important property, as it determines the type of data the field can store.

Data types can seem confusing; for example, if a field's data type is Short Text, it can store data that consists of text or numeric characters. However, a field whose data type is Number can only store numeric data. Therefore, you need to know which properties are used with each data type.

A field's data type determines many of its other qualities, including the following:

- formats that can be used with the field ;
- maximum value size ;
- how the field is used in expressions;
- whether or not the field can be indexed.

The data type of a field can be predefined, or you can select a data type depending on how you create the new field. For example, if you create a field in Datasheet mode and :

- if you use an existing field from another table, the data type is already defined in the model or in the other table.
- if you enter data in an empty column (or field), either Access assigns a data type to the field based on the values you enter, or you define the data type and format for the field yourself.
- Under the **Table fields** tab, in the **Add & Remove** group, click on **Other fields**, Access displays a list of data types you can select.

III.7. CONTROLS

Controls are the parts of a form or report that you use to enter, modify or display data.

Control types

Here's the list of control types you can use in Access desktop databases.

Control type	Notes
Text boxes	Use text box controls to display text, numbers, dates, times and memo fields. You can link a text box to one of the fields of an underlying table or query. If you let a text box linked to a field be updated, you can modify the value of the field in the underlying table or query by entering a new value in the text box. You can also use a text box to display calculated values.
Label	Use label controls that contain fixed text. By default, controls that can display data have a label control automatically attached. You can use this control to create stand-alone labels for titles and to

	obtain instructions on your form.
Control button	Use command button controls to activate a Visual Basic macro or procedure. You can also specify a hypertext link address that Access opens when a user clicks on the button.
Tab controls	Use tab controls to create a series of tab pages on your form. Each page can contain a number of other controls to display information. Tab controls work like most option dialogs or property sheet windows in Access . When a user clicks on another tab, Access displays the controls contained in that tab.
Link	Use the Link/Hypertext Link control option to add a hypertext link in a label control to your form creation grid. This hypertext link can contain a URL (Uniform Resource Locator) pointing to a location on the Internet, on a local intranet or on a local drive. It can also use a UNC (Universal Naming Convention) file name to point to a file on a server on your local area network (LAN) or on the drives of your local computer. The link can point to a file that is a web page or even another object in your current database. Click this button in the Ribbon Controls group to open the Insert Hypertext Link dialog box.
Web browser	Use a web browser control to display web page content directly inside a form. You can use a web browser control to display, for example, a map of an address stored in a table. You can link the web browser control to a field in your form's record source using the control's Source property. Note that you can't have a web browser control linked in the Details section of a continuous form.
Navigation	Use a navigation control to give you easy access to different forms and reports in your database. A navigation control provides an interface similar to that seen on websites, with buttons and tabs for navigating around a website. Note that you cannot have a navigation control in the Details section of a continuous form.
Option group	Use option group controls to contain one or more toggle buttons, radio buttons or checkboxes. (See the descriptions of these controls

	later in this table.) You can assign a separate numerical value to each button or checkbox you include in the group. When you have multiple buttons or checkboxes in a group, you can only select one button or checkbox at a time, and the value assigned to that button or checkbox becomes the value of the option group. If you have incorrectly assigned the same value to several buttons or checkboxes, all buttons or checkboxes with the same value appear highlighted when you click on one of them. You can select one of the group's buttons or checkboxes as the default value for the group. If you link the option group to a field in the underlying query or table, you can set a new value in the field by selecting a button or checkbox in the group.
Page break	Use a page break to separate the pages of a multi-page form.
Drop-down	Use a drop-down zone control to contain a list of potential values for the control and an editable text box. To create the list, you can enter values for the Drop-down box's Row Source property. You can also specify a table or query as the source of the list values. Access displays the currently selected value in the text box. When you click on the arrow to the right of the drop-down box, Access displays the values in the list. Select a new value from the list to reset the value in the control. If you link the drop-down list box to a field in the underlying table or query, you can modify the value of the field by selecting a new value from the list. If you link the drop-down box to a multiple-value field, Access displays the list with checkboxes to allow the user to select multiple values. You can link multiple columns to the list and hide one or more columns in the list by setting the column width to 0. You can link the actual value of the control to such a hidden column. When a multi-column list is closed, Access displays the value in the first column whose width is greater than 0. Access displays all non-zero width columns when you open the list.
Line	Use a row control to add rows to a form or report to enhance its

	appearance.
Toggle button	Use toggle controls to hold a value on/off, true/false or yes/no. When you click on a toggle button, its value changes to -1 (to represent on, true or yes), and the button appears depressed. Click the button again, its value changes to 0 (to represent off, false or no) and the button returns to normal. You can include a toggle button in an option group and assign the button a unique numerical value. If you create a group with multiple controls, selecting a new toggle button disables any previously selected toggle button, option button or checkbox in that group (unless other buttons or checkboxes in the group also have the same value). If you link the toggle button to a field in the underlying table or query, you can activate/deactivate the field value by clicking on the toggle button.
List box	Use a list zone control to contain a list of potential values for the control. To create the list, you can enter the values in the Line source property of the list box. You can also specify a table or query as the source of the list values. List fields are always open, and Access highlights the value currently selected in the list field. Selecting a new value in the list resets the value in the control. If you link the list box to a field in the underlying table or query, you can modify the field value by selecting a new value from the list. If you link the list box to a multiple-value field, Access displays the list with checkboxes to allow the user to select multiple values. You can link multiple columns to the list and hide one or more columns in the list by setting the width of a column to 0. You can link the actual value of the control to such a hidden column. Access displays all non-zero width columns corresponding to the control's defined width. If the list box control is independent, you can allow the user to select multiple values from the list (also known as a multi-select list box).
Rectangle	Use a rectangle control to add filled or empty rectangles to a form to enhance its appearance. You can use this control, for example, to visually group different controls.

Checkbox control	Use a checkbox control to maintain an on/off, true/false or yes/no value. When you activate a checkbox, its value changes to -1 (to represent on, true or yes), and a tick appears in the field. Activate the checkbox again and its value changes to 0 (to represent off, false or no), and the checkmark disappears from the field. You can include a checkbox in an option group and assign it a unique numerical value. If you create a group with multiple controls, activating a new checkbox disables any toggle buttons, radio buttons or checkboxes previously selected in that group (unless other buttons or checkboxes in the group also have the same value). If you link the checkbox to a field in the underlying table or query, you can activate/deactivate the field value by clicking on the checkbox.
frame	Use an independent object frame to add an object from another application that supports object linking and embedding (OLE). The object becomes part of your form, not part of the underlying table or query data. You can add images, sounds, graphics or slides to enhance your form. When the object is a chart, you can specify a query as the data source for the chart, and you can link the chart display to the active record in the form by one or more field values.
Attachment	Use an attachment control to link this to an attachment field in the underlying data. You can use this control, for example, to display an image or attach other files. In Form mode, this control presents the Manage Attachments dialog, where you can attach, delete and display multiple attachment files stored in the underlying field.
Radio button	Use a radio button control (sometimes called a radio button control) to hold a value on/off, true/false or yes/no. When you select a radio button, its value changes to -1 (to represent on, true or yes), and a filled circle appears in the center of the button. Select the button again, and its value becomes 0 (to represent off, false or no), and the filled circle disappears. You can include an option button in an option group and assign the button a unique numerical value. If you create a group with multiple controls, selecting a new radio button

	disables any previously selected toggle button, radio button or checkbox in that group (unless other buttons or checkboxes in the group also have the same value). If you link the radio button to a field in the underlying table or query, you can activate/deactivate the field value by clicking on the radio button.
Sub-form/sub-report	Use the sub-form/sub-report control to incorporate another form or report into the active form. You can use the sub-form or sub-report to display data from a table or query associated with the data in the main form. Access retains the link between the main form and the sub-form or sub-report for you.
Linked object frame	Use a linked object frame to display and modify an OLE object field from the underlying data. Access can display most images and graphics directly on a form. For other objects, Access displays the icon of the application in which the object was created. For example, if the object is a sound object created in Windows Sound Recorder, you'll see a speaker icon on your form.
Image	Use the image control to place a static image on your form. You can't modify the image on the form, but Access stores it in a format that's very efficient for the speed and size of the application. If you wish to use an image as the entire background of your form, you can set the form's Picture property.
Graphics	Use the Graphic control to add a graphic to your form grid. Click this button, then place the control on your form to start the Graphic Wizard, which guides you through the steps required to create a graphic.
ActiveX	Use the ActiveX control button to open a dialog box displaying all the ActiveX controls you have installed on your system. You can select one of the controls, then click OK to add it to the form grid. Not all ActiveX controls work with Access.

III.8. EASE OF USE

Unlike other database management systems, such as Oracle or my structured query language (MySQL), Microsoft Access is primarily designed for smaller-scale projects. It offers a more user-friendly interface and is suitable for individuals or small businesses who need to create and manage databases without in-depth technical knowledge. Access is often used for stand-alone desktop applications or collaboration between small teams, rather than for large-scale enterprise solutions.

III.9. LAYOUTS

Access creates the form and displays it in Layout mode. This mode allows you to make changes to the structure of the form while the data is still displayed. For example, you can adjust the size of text boxes to suit the data to be displayed, if required.

If Access finds a single table that has a one-to-many relationship with the table or query you've used to create the form, Access adds a data sheet to the form based on the associated table or query. For example, if you create a simple form based on the Employees table, and a one-to-many relationship is already defined between the Employees table and the Orders table, the data sheet displays all the records in the Orders table related to the current Employee record. If you don't need the data sheet, you can delete it from the form. If there are several tables with a one-to-many relationship with the table you used to create the form, Access does not add data sheets to the form.

III. 10.FORM PRESENTATION STYLES

Forms in Access are like store windows: it's easy to see or take the items you want. As forms are objects through which you or other users can add, modify or display data stored in your desktop Access database, form design is of particular importance. If your desktop Access database is to be used by several users, well-designed forms are essential for efficient and accurate data entry.

CHAPTER 4: REPORTS

IV. 1. CONCEPT DEFINITIONS

IV. 1.1 Reports

A report is a representation of the records in a database, which is printed out. It is possible to produce a synthesis from this data, which would otherwise be more difficult to obtain. It also makes it easier to sort and group information into relevant fields.

IV. 1.2.Reports

A report is a database object which is useful when you wish to present information from your database for one of the following uses: display or distribute a summary of data, archive snapshots of data, provide details on individual records, create labels.

IV. 1.3 Report labels

In Access, you create labels as a report, which is formatted with a small page size to fit the desired label. The most common use of labels is for direct mail, but all Access data can be printed in label format for a variety of purposes. In the case of mailing labels, the report obtains the address data from the tables or queries containing the addresses. Printing the report gives you a single label for each address in the underlying record source.

IV. 1.4. Add field

You can add fields to a form or report in the blink of an eye, using the **Field List** pane. When you double-click on a field in the **Field List** pane (or drag a field from the list to your form or report), Microsoft Access automatically creates the appropriate control to display the field there, for example, a text box or checkbox, and then links the control to that field.

Add a control to a form or report using the Control List pane

1. Open your report in Page or Create mode.

   If the **Field List** pane is not displayed, do one of the following:

   - In the **Creation** tab, in the **Tools** group, click on **Add existing fields**.

-OR-

- Press Alt+F8.

2. In the **Field list** pane, find the table containing the field you wish to add. To show or hide the list of fields for each table, click on the plus (+) or minus (**-**) sign next to the table name.

   Note: If the database contains no tables, the **Field List** pane is empty.

3. When you find the field you want to add, do one of the following to add it to the form or report:
   - Double-click on the field.
   - Drag the field from the **Field List** pane to the form or report.
   - To add several fields at once, hold down the Ctrl key and click on several fields, then drag them all to the form or report.

     Note: You can only use this technique on fields listed in the **Fields available for this view** section of the **Field List** pane.

   - To add a range of fields from the **Field List** pane to the form or report, proceed as follows:
   - Click on the first field in the range.
   - Hold down the Shift key, then click on the last field in the range.

     Access selects the two fields you clicked on, plus all the fields in between.

   - Drag all selected fields to the form or report.

     Note: You can only use this technique on fields listed in the **Fields available for this view** section of the **Field List** pane.

4. Access creates the appropriate control to display each field and also links the control to the field. In addition, Access creates a label associated with the control. You can modify the label by clicking on it once to select it, then clicking on it again to place the insertion point in the label. You can then edit the label in the

same way as you would edit text in a document.

5. If you want a field to be displayed in a control type other than the one Access has automatically created, you can change the control type. However, you can only replace it with a control type appropriate to that field. For example, you can replace an editable list box with a text box or a list box, but not with a command button.

   Changing the type of control used

   a. Open the form or report in Design mode by right-clicking on it in the in the navigation pane, then clicking on **Create mode**.
   b. Right-click on the control to be modified, then click on **Replace with**.

      If the **Replace with** menu item is not available, this means that no other control type is suitable for this field. Otherwise, Access displays a list of available control types.

   c. Click on one of them to use that control type instead of the other.

      The control remains linked to the field, but you may need to set certain properties to make the new control type work the way you want it to. To display a control's property sheet, click on the control to select it, then press F4.

Adding a control to a form or report without using the Field List pane

As a general rule, the quickest way to add a control to a form or report is to use the Field List pane. However, you can also add a control by creating a control and linking it to the control. The following steps explain how to do this:

1. In the navigation pane, right-click on the form or report, then click on **Page Mode** or **Create Mode**.

   Control Wizards You can use Control Wizards to create command buttons, list fields, sub-forms, editable list fields and option groups. A Control Wizard asks you a series of questions about how you want the control to look and work, then creates the control and defines its properties based on your answers. In the **Creation** tab, in the **Controls** group, click on the down arrow next to the control gallery. If the **Use Control Wizards** option is not activated, click on it.

On the other hand, if you prefer to create controls without the help of Wizards, click on the **Use Control Wizards** option to deactivate it.

2. In the **Creation** tab, in the **Controls** group, click on the tool corresponding to the type of control you wish to add.

   To determine the name of a tool, position the pointer over it. Access displays the tool name.

3. In the form or report creation grid, click on the position where you wish to the top left-hand corner of the control. Click once to create a default-sized control, or click on the tool and drag the selection in the form grid to create a control of the desired size.
4. If you have activated the **Use Control Wizards** option and the control you are positioning has a Wizard associated with it, the Wizard starts and guides you through the control configuration.
5. If you don't position the control perfectly on the first attempt, you can move it as follows:
   a. Click on the control to select it. If a label is associated with the control, hold down the Ctrl key and click on the label to select it too.
   b. Position the pointer over the control until it changes to a + movement pointer.
   c. Click and drag the control to the desired location.

IV. 1.5 Calculated fields

In Access, you can create table fields that calculate values. Calculations can include values from fields in the same table, as well as Access built-in functions.

These calculated fields can be added to tables, queries, forms or reports.

Notes :

- The calculation cannot include fields from other tables or queries.
- Calculation results are read-only.
- Calculated fields are only available in Access databases using the .accdb file format.
- You need Access 2010 or later.

Create a calculated field in table data sheet mode

1. Open the table by double-clicking on it in the navigation pane.
2. Scroll horizontally to the rightmost column in the table, then click on the **Click to add** column header.
3. In the list that appears, click on **Calculated field**, then click on the desired data type for the result. Access displays the Expression Generator.
4. Start typing the desired calculation for this field. For example: [Quantity] * [Unit price].

   Note: An equal sign (=) is not required before the expression.

5. Click **OKAccess** adds the calculated field, then highlights the field header so you can type in a field name.
6. Type a name for the calculated field, then press Enter.

Modifying a calculated field in table data sheet mode

1. Open the table by double-clicking on it in the navigation pane.
2. Click on the calculated field you wish to modify.
3. Under the **Fields** tab, in the **Properties** group, click on **Modify PExpression**. Access displays the Expression Generator.
4. In the expression field, make the necessary changes to the calculation.

   Note: It is not necessary to precede the expression with an equal sign (=).

5. Click on OK.

IV. 1.6.Summary fields

Reports provide a means of displaying, formatting and summarizing the information in your Microsoft Access database. For example, you can create a simple report of the telephone numbers of all your contacts, or a summary report of total sales in different regions at different periods.

IV.2. REPORT TYPES

Standard	To show database records in report form.
Graph	To graphically represent database records.
Labels	To prepare labels for mailing or conference purposes.

IV. 3.REPORT CREATION MODES

Access lets you create all kinds of reports, from the simplest to the most complex. Start by thinking about the source of your report. Whether your report is a simple list of records or a grouped summary of sales by region, you need to start by determining which fields contain the data you want to display in your report, and in which tables or queries.

IV.3.1 Creating a report using the Report tool

The Report tool is the fastest way to create a report, as it generates it immediately, without asking for any information. The report displays all the fields in the underlying table or query. The Report tool may not create the polished final report you want, but it's very useful for quickly viewing the underlying data. You can then save the report and modify it in Page or Create mode to suit your needs.

1. In the navigation pane, click on the table or query on which you wish to base the report.
2. In the **Create** tab, in the **Reports** group, click on **Report**.

Access generates the report and displays it in Page mode.

Once you've viewed the report, you can save it, then close it and the underlying table or query you've used as a record source. The next time you open the report, Access will display the most recent data from your record source.

IV. 3.2 Creating a report using the Report Wizard

The Report Wizard lets you be more selective about the fields that appear in the report. You can also specify how data is grouped and sorted, and use fields from several tables or queries, provided you have previously defined the relationships between tables and queries.

- In the **Create** tab, in the **Report** group, click on **Report Wizard.**
- Follow the instructions provided on the Report Wizard pages. On the last page, click

page, click on **Finish.**

When you preview the report, you'll see it as it will appear when printed. You can also increase the zoom factor to enlarge details.

Note: If you wish to include fields from several tables or queries in the report, do not click **Next** or **Finish** after selecting the fields from the first table or query on the first page of the Report Wizard. Instead, repeat the steps for selecting a table or query, then click on the other fields to be included in the report. Click **Next** or **Finish** to continue.

IV. 3.3 Creating labels with the Label Wizard

The Label Wizard helps you to easily create labels for a wide range of standard label sizes.

1. In the navigation pane, double-click to open the table or query from which you want to save your labels.
2. In the **Create** tab, in the **Reports** group, click on **Labels.**
3. Follow the instructions on the Label Wizard pages. On the last
   last page, click on **Finish.**

Access displays your labels in Print Preview mode, so you can see them as they will appear when printed. You can use the cursor control on the Access status bar to zoom in on details.

Note: Print preview is the only display mode that allows you to see multiple columns. The other display modes show data in a single column.

IV. 3.4 Creating a report using the Blank Report tool

If you don't want to use the Report Tool or Report Wizard, you can use the Blank Report Tool to create a report from scratch. This can enable you to create a report very quickly, especially if you only intend to place a few fields in the report. The following procedure explains how to use the Blank Report tool:

- On the **Create** tab, in the **Reports** group, click on **Blank report**.

  A blank report is displayed in Page mode, with the Field List pane appearing on the right-hand side of the Access window.

- In the **Field List** pane, click on the plus sign (+) next to the tables containing the fields to be displayed on the report.
- Drag and drop each field successively onto the report, or select several fields while holding down the Ctrl key, then drag and drop them onto the report at the same time.
- Use the tools in the **Header/Footer** group of **the Report Creation** tab to add a logo, title, page numbers or the date and time of the report.

IV. 4.REPORT STRUCTURE

The report consists of the following parts:

Report header: this part appears only once, at the start of the report.

Page header: appears at the beginning of each page of the report.

Group header: checks have been grouped by issuing bank. The group header includes the bank name ("Bank" field). It is modified each time the bank is changed.

Detail: this line contains the fields that will appear in the report.

Group footer: this shows the total number of cheques issued by bank.

Page footer: at the bottom of each page.

Report footer: appears only once, at the end of the report. In this case, it shows the grand total of checks issued.

IV. 5.ROLE OF A REPORT

Reports provide a means of displaying, formatting and summarizing the information in your Microsoft Access database. For example, you can create a simple report of telephone numbers for all your contacts, or a summary report of total sales in different regions at different times.

IV. 6. DIFFERENT PRINT MODES

To print a report without previewing it :

- Right-click on the report in the navigation pane and click on **Print**. The report is sent to your default printer.

  Note: If you select the report in the navigation pane and click **Print** in the **File** tab, you can select further print options, such as page numbers and number of copies, and specify a printer.

  - To open a dialog box in which you can select a printer, specify the number of copies and set other parameters, click **Print**.

IV. 7.PRINT OPTIONS

If you are able to print the data from a table, query, form or report in your Microsoft Access database, you can define report print options to produce a nice, more readable printed copy of your data.

Printing data directly from tables or queries works when you want to print a simple list. Forms are best suited to displaying or printing data for a single record or a linked set of records, rather than for printing large datasets or data summaries. Printing report data allows you to compare, summarize and sum large data sets, then present this information in an attractive format.

IV. 7.1 Select page configuration options

Once you've created your report, you can set page setup options in the **Page Setup** dialog box. These options allow you to adjust the format with options for margin settings, to use grids and columns, or to print only the report data without formatting. To set page printing options, proceed as follows:

1. In the navigation pane, right-click on the report, then click on **Print preview**.

2. On the **Print Preview** tab, in the **Page Setup** group, click **Page Setup** and define the margins, orientation and column settings of your choice.

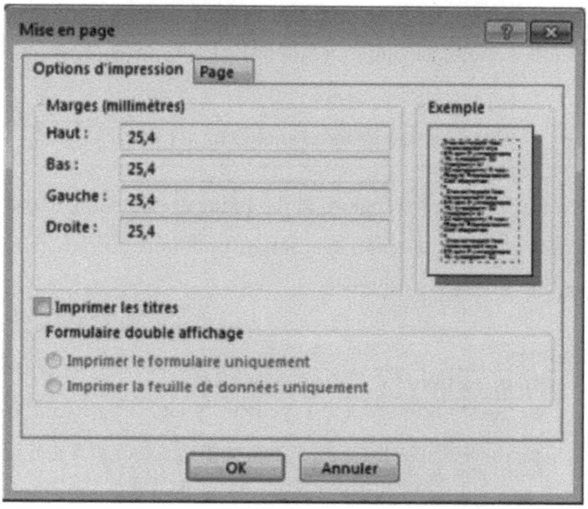

Print Options tab parameters

Parameter	Description
Margins (inches)	Increase or decrease default margins as required and see changes displayed in the **preview** page.
Data only	Select this option if you do not wish to print layout features in the report, such as grids.
Dual view form	If this option is not available for a report :

To customize the margins on your report, in the **Print preview** tab, in the **Page size** group, click on **Margins** and select an appropriate option. A preview of the report with the modified margin settings is displayed.

Page tab **parameters**

Parameter	Description
Orientation	Select Portrait or Landscape orientation. If you want to see how the report is displayed, rather than setting the orientation here, set it via the Page Preview tab. On the **Print Preview** tab, in the **Page Setup** group, click on **Portrait** or **Landscape**.
Paper	Select paper size and source.
Printer for List of con...	If you select **Use specific printer**, you can define several other printer and document size options.

Columns tab settings

Note: These options are also available on the **Print Preview** tab, in the **Page Setup** group, under **Columns**.

Parameter	Description
Grid settings	Select number of columns and spacing between rows. If the setting applies to a single column, the **Column spacing** and **Column format** options will not be available.
As Detail section	Select this option to print the column at the same size as defined in the report. To adjust column height and width, deactivate the selection and enter new values.
Column size	Select column width and height.
Column format	Select the direction in which you wish columns to be printed. This

	option is available if you have at least two columns.

IV. 7.2 Select printer parameters

Once you've defined your report's page setup parameters, you can select specific print options to control the layout or pages you want to print and the number of copies.

1. In the navigation pane, right-click on the report, then click on **Print preview**.

2. Click **Print preview**, then in the **Print** group, click **Print**.

   Keyboard shortcut Press Ctrl+P.

3. Select your print options, then click **OK** to print your report.

The following table describes the results you can expect from specific print parameters:

Parameter	Description
Printer	Select the printer on which you wish to print the report. If you have not defined paper orientation and size, click on the **Properties** button.
Print	• To print only selected pages of the report, select **Pages** and define the range. For example, to print only page 5 of a report, type **5** in the **From** and **To** fields. • To print one page of your report, set the **From** and **To** fields to the same page number.
Copies	Select the number of copies, then **Collate copies** if you want to print copies in groups for a multi-page report.

To save paper, send a print job to a commercial printer or e-mail the report, you can create a .pdf or xps format of your report: in the **Print Preview** tab, in the **Data** group, click on **PDF or XPS**.

IV. 7.3 Print preview

Use the Print preview option to check the appearance of the printed version of your report.

You can open a report in the print preview as follows:

- To preview a report that is not already open, right-click on it in the navigation pane.

  navigation pane, right-click on the report you wish to preview, then click **Print preview**.

  or

- Click on **File**> **Print**, then on **Print Preview**.

  or

- If the report is open, right-click on the report's document tab, then click on **Print Preview**.

You can make further formatting changes from the Print Preview by using the options on the Print **Preview** tab.

If you wish to view multiple pages of the report, access other pages or view multiple pages at the same time when previewing your report, try one of the following options:

- Click on the **Open/Close Resize Bar** button (<<) in the top right-hand corner of the navigation pane, then expand the report display area.
- Position the report using the horizontal or vertical scrollbars.
- To enlarge an area of the report, in the **Print Preview** tab, in the **Zoom** group, click on the arrow under **Zoom** and select an enlargement percentage. You can also use the Zoom control in the bottom right-hand corner of your window.
- To preview several pages at once, in the **Zoom** group, click on **Two pages** or **More pages** , then select an option.

Select your print options: In the **Print** group, click on **Print** , then select your print options.

Close print preview: In the **Close preview** group, click on **Close print preview**.

IV. 8.EXTERNAL DATA

IV.8.1 Importing data

There are two ways of importing Access data into Excel:

- Import directly from Excel.
- Export data from Access to Excel.

Although, at first glance, these two techniques seem to produce the same results, there are certain nuances between them. It may therefore be that one is preferable to the other.

Importing Access data from Excel

This method has the advantage of not requiring you to own Access, but can sometimes slightly change the wording of headers, or the order in which data rows are displayed. In addition, this method offers greater choice as to how the data should be processed in Excel.

To import Access data via Excel :

1. Go to the Data ribbon and select ***Access*** in ***External data.***

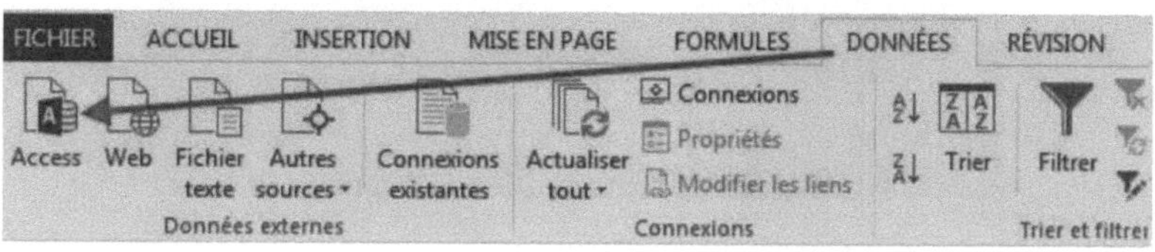

2. Select the Access file you wish to import data from.
3. Select the data table(s) in the file to be imported.

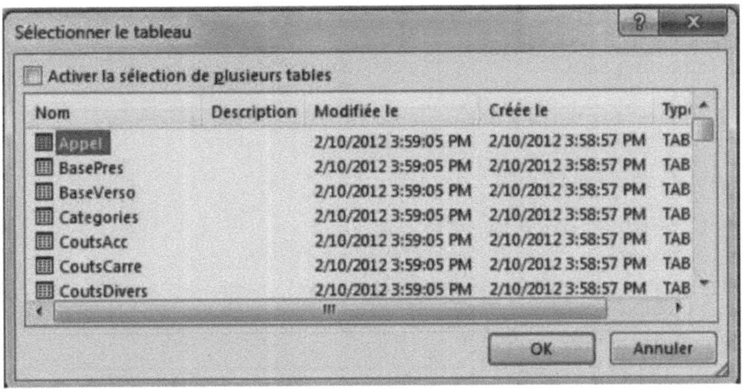

4. Select the import format (Table is the most common database format).

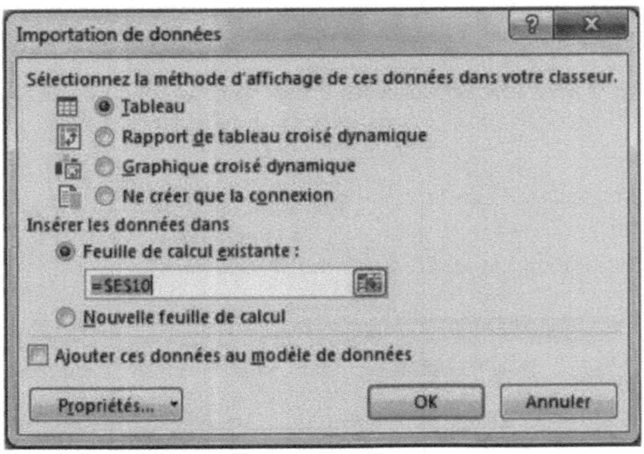

5. Choose where to import Access data into the Excel file.

IV.8.2 Exporting data

This method has the advantage of ensuring that the database retains exactly the same appearance as the one in Access once the export to Excel has been completed (i.e. the import of Access data into Excel). However, this method requires Microsoft Access.

To export Access data to Excel from Microsoft Access :

1. Open the Access file.
2. Select the data table to be exported.

3. Go to the ***External Data*** ribbon and select ***Excel*** in the ***Export*** section of the ribbon (right-clicking on the data table also offers export choices).

4. Choose where to save the resulting Excel file.

IV.9. DATABASE SECURITY

Access provides an enhanced security model designed to simplify the application of security procedures to a database, and the opening of a secure database.

Here's what's new in Access security:

What's new in version 2010

- **New encryption technology** Office 2010 offers a new, more powerful encryption technology than that offered by Office 2007.
- **Support for third-party encryption products** Access 2010 lets you use a third-party encryption technology if you prefer. This article does not cover the use of third-party products.

What's new in version 2007

- **Ability to view data even when you don't want to activate the database content** In Microsoft Office Access 2003, if you chose the "High" security level, you had to code-sign and approve a database before you could view its data. Now you can view the data without having to decide whether or not to approve the database.
- **Greater ease of use** If you place database files (either in the new

in the new Access file format, or in previous file formats) in an approved location (such as a folder or network share that you designate as secure), these files will open and run without displaying a warning message, or asking you to activate any disabled content. In addition, if you open databases created with previous versions of Access (such as .mdb or .mde files) in Access 2010, and these databases have been digitally signed and you have chosen to trust the publisher, these files will run without any intervention on your part. However, remember that the VBA code for a signed database will not run until you have approved the editor, and will not run if the digital signature becomes invalid. This can happen when someone (who hasn't signed the database) modifies the contents of the database.

- **Trusted Relationship Center** The Privacy Management Center is a dialog box that provides a single location for defining and modifying Access security settings. You will use the Privacy Management Center to create or modify trusted locations, and to set security options for Access. These settings influence the behavior of existing or new databases when they are opened in this version of Access. In addition, the Privacy Management Center includes procedures for evaluating the components of a database, and determining whether it can be opened safely, or whether the Privacy Management Center should disable it and leave the decision to activate it to you.
- **Fewer error messages** Previous versions of Access included numerous warning messages

numerous warning messages: macro security and sandbox mode, to name but two. By default, if you open an .accdb file that you haven't already approved, you'll only see a single tool called the Message Bar.

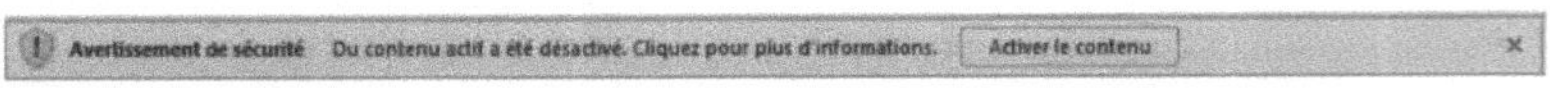

If you want to trust a database, you can use the Message Bar to activate any disabled database content (action queries [queries that add, delete or modify data], macros, ActiveX controls, expressions

[functions that evaluate a single value] and VBA code) when you open a database that contains one or more of these components.

- **New methods for signing and distributing database files**

  In Access versions prior to 2007, you used Visual Basic Editor to apply a security certificate to individual database components. Now, you create a database package, then sign and distribute it.

If you extract a database from a signed package in an approved location, the database opens without displaying the message bar. If you extract a database from a signed package in an unapproved location, but have approved the package certificate and signature, the database runs without displaying the message bar.

Note: When you create a package and sign an unapproved database or one that contains an invalid digital signature, you must use the message bar to approve the database each time it is opened, unless you place it in an approved location.

- **More powerful algorithm for encrypting databases in .accdb file format that use database password functionality** Encrypting a database scrambles the data in your tables, and prevents unauthorized users from reading your data.

Note: When you encrypt a database with a password, the encrypted database uses page-level locking regardless of your application settings. This can affect data availability in a shared environment.

- **New subclass of macro actions that run when a database is deactivated** These more secure macros also contain error handling functions. You can also integrate macros (even those containing actions disabled by Access) directly into a form, report or control property that would work logically with a VBA code module or macro from a previous version of Access.

Finally, don't forget to observe the following rules:

- If you open a database in an approved location, all components are activated without any security decision on your part.
- If you create, sign and distribute a database package with an older file format (.mdb or .mde file), all components are activated without the need for security decisions if the database contains a valid digital signature obtained from an approved publisher and you approve the certificate.
- If you sign and distribute an unapproved database from an unapproved location, the Privacy Management Center deactivates the database by default, and you must choose to activate the database each time you open it.

Access and user-level security

Access does not support user-level security for databases created with the new file formats (.accdb and .accde files). However, if you open a database created with a previous version of Access in Access 2010 and user-level security is applied to this database, these settings will still be active.

Important : Permissions created using user-level security functionality do not protect your database against malicious users, and are not designed to act as a security barrier. This feature is suitable for enhancing the use of a database by approved users. To ensure the security of your data, use Windows file system permissions to authorize only approved users to access your database file or associated user-level security files.

If you convert a database from a previous version of Access with user-level security to the new file format, Access automatically removes all security settings and the security rules of the .accdb or .accde files apply.

Remember that all users can see all database objects at any time when you open databases in the new file format.

Access security architecture

To understand Access security architecture, you need to bear in mind that an Access database is not an Excel workbook or Word document. In fact, an Access database is a collection of objects (tables, forms, queries, macros, reports, etc.) which are often interdependent. For example, if you create a data entry form, you can't enter or store data in that form unless you've associated (linked) the form controls to a table.

Several Access components can present security risks and are therefore disabled in an approved database:

- Action queries (queries that insert, delete or modify data) ;
- macros ;
- certain expressions (functions that return a single value) ;
- VBA code.

To make your data even more secure, Access and the Privacy Management Center perform a series of security tests each time a database is opened. The procedure is as follows:

- When you open an .accdb or .accde file, Access submits the database location to the

Privacy Management Center. If it determines that the location is approved, the database runs with full functionality. If you open a database in a previous file format, Access submits the file location and digital signature details to the Privacy Management Center.

The Privacy Management Center checks these "facts" to assess the reliability of the database, and then tells Access how to open the database. Access then decides whether to deactivate the database or open it with full functionality.

Note: Remember that the settings you or your system administrator choose in the Privacy Management Center determine the privacy decisions applicable when opening databases.

For more information on using the Privacy Management Center, see the section **See also**.

- If the Privacy Management Center disables database content, the message bar is displayed when the database is opened.

To enable database content, click on **Options** and choose the appropriate options in the dialog box that appears. Access activates the deactivated content and the database reopens with full functionality. Otherwise, the deactivated components will not function.

- If you open a database created with an older file format (.mdb or .mde files) and this database is neither signed nor trusted, Access disables all executable content by default.

CHAPTER 5: ARTIFICIAL INTELLIGENCE (EXPERT SYSTEM)

V. 1.DEFINITION

V. 1.1 Artificial intelligence

Artificial intelligence is a set of theories and techniques used to create machines capable of simulating human intelligence.

V. 1.2. Algorithms

Algorithms are the principles, rules and techniques used to write an algorithm.

V. 1.3 Algorithm

An algorithm is a sequence of operations, called **instructions**, to be carried out in order to achieve a goal (solve a problem, cook a dish, make a robot move, etc.). These instructions are said to be **executed.**

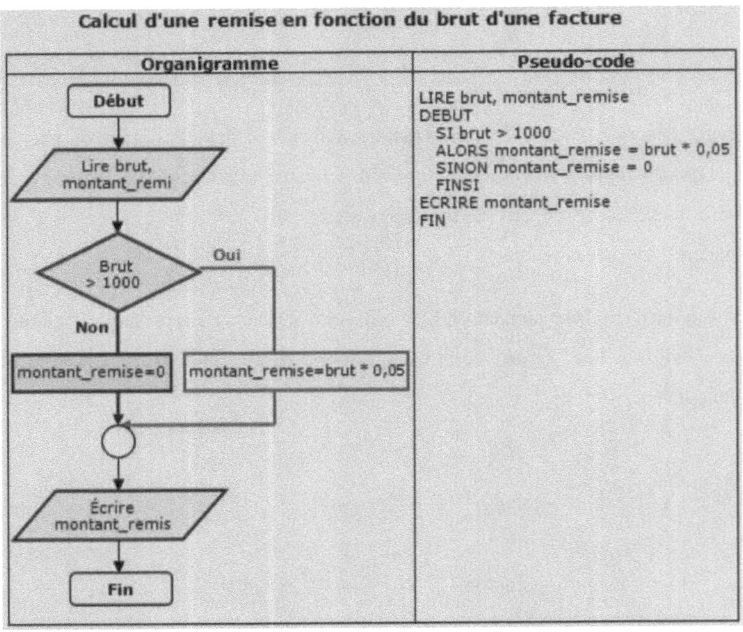

V. 2. ALGORITHMS AND ARTIFICIAL INTELLIGENCE

An algorithm is a detailed set of instructions and procedures designed to solve a problem or accomplish a particular task. In terms of artificial intelligence, algorithms are often used to describe the methods used by machine learning models to solve complex tasks.

Algorithms can be implemented as computer programs that follow instructions using inputs to produce outputs. Algorithms can be described in different ways, such as formal programming algorithms or algorithms described informally in the form of pseudocode or flowcharts.

There are many different algorithms used in the fields of AI and signal processing, such as regression algorithms, classification algorithms, pattern recognition algorithms and speech recognition algorithms. The algorithms chosen for a given task depend on many factors, such as data properties, model goals and available computing resources.

V. 2.1 Types of algorithms used in AI

In artificial intelligence (AI), different types of algorithms are used, depending on the problem to be solved, the data available and the context in which the solution will be applied. Some of the main types of algorithm used in AI are as follows:

1. **Supervised learning algorithms**
   - **Linear and logistic regression**. Used to predict a continuous or categorical variable, respectively.
   - **Support vector machines (SVM)**. For classification and regression on complex data.
   - **Decision trees and random forests**. Used in classification and regression, and famous for its interpretability.
2. **Unsupervised learning algorithms**
   - **Clustering (K-Means, Hierarchical)**. For grouping unlabeled data into *clusters* or groups.
   - **Principal component analysis (PCA)**. To reduce data dimensionality.
3. **Reinforcement learning algorithms**
   - **Q-Learning, Deep Q Network (DQN)**. Used to teach agents how to act in an environment in order to maximize some notion of cumulative reward.

4. **Deep learning algorithms**
   - **Convolutional neural networks (CNN).** Particularly powerful in computer vision tasks.
   - **Recurrent neural networks (RNN), long-term memory (LSTM).** Used in natural language processing and time series.
   - **transformers.** Like BERT and GPT, used in text understanding and generation.
5. **Optimization algorithms**
   - **Gradual descent.** Used to optimize loss functions in many machine learning algorithms.
6. **Recommendation algorithms**
   - **Collaborative filtering, matrix factorization.** Used in recommender systems such as those found on e-commerce and entertainment platforms.
7. **Anomaly detection algorithms**
   - **Single-class SVM, isolation forest.** To detect abnormal patterns in data, such as fraud in financial transactions.
8. **Rule- and knowledge-based algorithms**
   - **Expert systems.** Use a knowledge base and rules to mimic the decision-making of experts in a specific field.
9. **hybrid and *ensemble* algorithms**

- **Stacking, bagging, boosting.** They combine several models to improve accuracy and robustness.

These algorithms represent only a fraction of the techniques available in AI. The choice of which algorithm or combination of algorithms to use depends largely on the specific problem, the data available and the particular requirements of the project, such as accuracy, interpretability and efficiency.

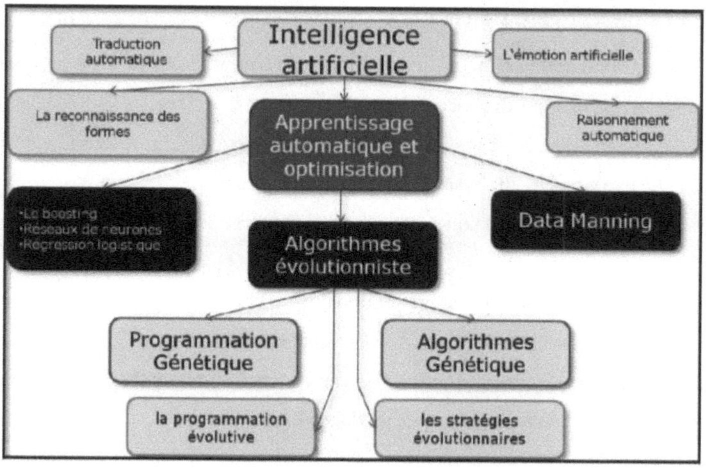

V. 3. EXPERT SYSTEMS

V. 3.1 Definition

An expert system is a software package whose ability to solve new problems in a given field is comparable to that of a human expert specializing in that field.

Artificial intelligence is booming today, with the boom in generative AI and LLMs (large language models) such as **GPT** or **Google Gemini**. However, this technology is far from new.

As early as the 1970s, the first concrete implementations were completed. It was at this time that computer scientist **Edward Feigenbaum of Stanford University** invented programs capable of solving complex problems by imitating the reasoning of human experts in a particular field: expert systems.

Although limited to restricted fields of knowledge, these systems offer the possibility of capitalizing on and disseminating the rare expertise of specialists.

Even today, they are **used in many sectors, including medicine, finance, industry and fault diagnosis**.

V. 3.2 How an expert system works

The general architecture of an expert system comprises three main components: the **knowledge base**, the **inference engine** and the **user interface**.

Firstly, the knowledge base contains **all domain knowledge**, represented in such a way that it can be exploited by the system.

The main representation techniques are production rules, objects, frames and semantic networks.

For example, in a medical system, symptoms, illnesses and their relationships can be represented by rules such as "If fever AND persistent cough, then flu".

At the heart of the system, the inference engine applies **algorithms** to deduce new knowledge from that contained in the knowledge base.

There are two main types of engine: **forward chaining** (from cause to effect) and **backward chaining** (from effect to cause). However, there are also mixed methods that combine these two approaches.

So, like humans, **expert systems can improve their performance** by gaining experience over time.

For its part, the user interface **enables communication between the human expert and the system**. It is as useful for acquiring knowledge as it is for executing the system or explaining its reasoning.

V. 3.3 Importance and fields of application of expert systems

The use of expert systems goes far beyond simple data processing tools. Their **ability to reproduce and apply human expertise** is proving useful for a multitude of applications in various sectors.

In the medical field, they are used to diagnose and treat disease. **They analyze symptoms reported by patients**, compare this data with a comprehensive medical knowledge base , and provide recommendations to healthcare professionals.

In addition, they can be used to **plan personalized treatments** based on a patient's specific characteristics.

In engineering, expert systems are deployed to **help design, maintain and troubleshoot**

complex systems.

This includes power grids, industrial control systems and critical infrastructures. Their ability to **identify potential problems, propose solutions and proactively optimize the process** makes them invaluable tools.

In the financial sector, these systems are used for risk assessment, portfolio management, fraud detection and investment decision-making.

Their **ability to analyze large quantities of financial data in real time** and provide recommendations based on predefined models and rules makes them indispensable for financial institutions.

They are also widely used in industry for quality control, predictive maintenance, supply chain management and manufacturing process optimization.

By **identifying potential problems, diagnosing faults and proposing solutions in real time**, they help to improve operational efficiency and reduce costs.

In a wide variety of contexts, expert systems can be used as **decision-support tools**. This is the case for human resources management, logistics and strategic planning.

Decision-makers can rely on their analysis of complex data, **their identification of trends or their recommendations for** appropriate **action** to make the best choices and anticipate future challenges.

V. 3.4. The best-known expert systems

Among the most widely used and reputed expert systems, we can cite several examples. **CaDet (Cancer Decision Support Tool)** can identify cancer in its earliest stages.

Similarly, **PXDES** can determine the type and severity of a patient's lung cancer. Doctors can also rely on DXplain to diagnose various diseases.

They can also use **MYCIN** to identify bacteria such as bacteremia and meningitis. **DENDRAL**, meanwhile, helps chemists identify unknown biological molecules.

In manufacturing, the **R1/XCON** expert system automatically selects and orders computer components based on customer specifications.

V. 3.5 Advantages and limitations of expert systems

The main advantage of expert systems is that they **enable expertise to be disseminated on a large scale, reduce costs compared with the use of human experts, and support decision-making** in critical areas.

Without replacing human experts, they can complement them by **making decisions based on rules and facts** rather than emotional influence.

What's more, unlike humans who may decide to leave their jobs, expert systems retain their knowledge and information permanently.

Nevertheless, these systems also have important limitations. **Their field of knowledge is restricted to a particular domain**, defined during development. As a result, any new situation outside this framework cannot be handled correctly by the system.

We can also deplore their overly linear way of thinking and their inability to truly solve problems. **They are also sorely lacking in human intuition, and their lack of emotion can also be a weakness** in certain cases, such as announcing a medical diagnosis to a patient.

Another major challenge is maintenance. As knowledge is constantly evolving, the knowledge base needs to be updated regularly. This is a time-consuming and costly process. What's more, certain types of complex knowledge pose difficulties for their formal representation in expert systems. This is the case, for example, with **reasoning by**

analogy.

V. 3.6. Modern expert systems and AI

In the past, the first expert systems relied essentially on rule bases defined by human experts. This is no longer the case.

Recent advances in AI, particularly in the field of Machine Learning, have made it possible to develop **new approaches**.

Today, **so-called "hybrid" expert systems** combine classic knowledge representation techniques with ML algorithms capable of automatically extracting patterns and rules from very large quantities of data.

The emergence of Big Data and massive processing technologies, such as Cloud Computing, has opened up **new perspectives for expert systems**. They can now draw on gigantic volumes of real data.

However, despite these important advances, **today's expert systems remain narrow or weak AI systems**, specialized on specific tasks.

Many challenges still lie ahead if we are to create general AI, capable of reasoning like humans about all kinds of problems...

V. 3.7. Developing an expert system: the steps to follow

The development of an expert system begins with the **acquisition of knowledge from human experts in the field**.

This crucial stage involves a variety of techniques, such as interviews, analysis of existing documentation, and observation of experts in problem-solving situations.

Once the knowledge has been acquired, it needs to be modeled and represented in a **formalism that can be understood by the system** (rules, objects, frames...).

This process often involves **simplifying and structuring the** experts' sometimes incomplete or imprecise **knowledge**.

Once these steps have been completed and the system is ready for use, it undergoes **a thorough validation** and **testing phase**.

Knowledge is verified, real-life cases are submitted and the system's reasoning is analyzed for errors and inconsistencies.

V. 4. IA DOMAINS

1. The Turing test

The Turing test is a proposed artificial intelligence test based on a machine's ability to imitate human conversation.

The principle of the Turing test: a human, called a judge, exchanges written messages via a computer keyboard with a human and a machine. The messages can be on any subject. The judge's objective is to determine which of his interlocutors is the human and which is the machine. The machine will be considered intelligent if it is able to deceive the judge in at least half the cases.

This is much more difficult than it sounds. The machine may give the illusion for a while or on certain subjects, but basic or even very simple questions can reveal the "deception". For example, ask the hidden interlocutor to perform a complicated operation such as dividing two large numbers. If the response time is too fast, it can easily betray the machine. The computer program needs to understand that the question being asked is difficult, if not impossible for a human, and feign slowness or ignorance. Humor and empathy can also be used to trick the machine.

2. Vision

Vision is the association between the sense of sight and a set of cognitive processes for which we need to use our brain.

The **eyes** only serve to pick up the signal contained in the light rays that strike the retinas, and never to extract information from them. They are part of a much more complete and complex whole. The **visual cortex** is part of this whole, and is the area of the **brain** that extracts the information. This information is then decoded and analyzed by other parts of the brain.

Computer vision, also known as **artificial vision** or **computer vision**, is a branch of artificial intelligence whose main aim is to enable a machine to "see" and eventually "recognize". The objectives of this field are the analysis, processing, interpretation and understanding of images taken by acquisition systems, be they sensors, spectrum analyzers, cameras or any other process.

Computer vision can be totally different from human vision. It is based on electronic components and therefore no longer has the physical limitations of human vision.

This vision can be wide-field like some birds, faceted like some insects, nocturnal, broad-spectrum with the possibility of seeing all kinds of frequencies, all kinds of color variations, or with very fine granularity enabling microscopic details to be seen.

Computer vision can be divided into **sub-fields**, each with its own research focus. The main ones **today** are

- **Image acquisition**: the design and development of the electronic components required for vision (cameras of all kinds, sensors, motion detectors, electronic components, etc.).
- **Image analysis and recognition**: this enables the recognition of faces, body parts, humans, etc.

3. Robotics

The common name **robotics** comes from the English word "robotics", coined by the Russian-born American novelist **Isaac Asimov** and popularized by a book published in 1942 (Runaround, Astounding Science Fiction, March 1942) in which he describes the three laws of robotics that are still considered today. The origin of the word **robot** comes from the Czech language, in which "robota" means forced labor.

L'ATILF's definition of a robot is as follows: "A device which, thanks to a microprocessor-based automatic control system, performs a precise task for which it has been designed, in the industrial, scientific, military or domestic domain".

It is thus possible to imagine two types of robotics:

- **Physical robotics**, made up of machines and sensors, managed by algorithms enabling it to be more or less autonomous in the tasks it performs.
- **Virtual robotics**, where robots can be virtual assistants, or logical robots capable of performing a number of actions automatically.

This section focuses on physical robotics, virtual assistants having been described earlier in this chapter. I will therefore consider the whole range of scientific and industrial fields related to the design and realization of robots.

Asimov's three laws:

Law 1: a robot may not harm a human being or, by remaining passive, allow a human being to be exposed to danger.

Law 2: a robot must obey orders given to it by a human being, unless such orders conflict with the first law.

Law 3: a robot must protect its own existence, as long as this protection does not conflict with...

4. Knowledge

Knowledge management and reasoning are one of the oldest branches of artificial intelligence, the aim being to enable a machine to access knowledge, reason and deduce.

We all have in mind the following example of reasoning (inference), which has been the basis of our expert systems.

- Every man is mortal.
- Socrates is a man.
- The machine then infers, without ever having had direct information, that Socrates is mortal.

a. Knowledge management

Knowledge Management (KM) is an artificial intelligence discipline whose aim is to use knowledge in the most complete and relevant way possible. It includes methods and software tools for identifying and capitalizing on knowledge, in order to organize, disseminate and use it.

Where does knowledge come from?

Knowledge comes from many sources, both structured and unstructured. As defined by **Nonaka** and **Takeuchi**, two experts in knowledge management, we generally distinguish **two forms of knowledge**:

- **Tangible knowledge**, also known as **explicit** knowledge. This is formalized, stored knowledge that can be "easily" retrieved by a system. It generally comes from information stored in databases, electronic or non-electronic documents, photos, videos, sound sequences, etc.
- **Intangible knowledge**, also known as knowledge...

5. Automatic planning and scheduling

This is a branch of artificial intelligence concerned with **scheduling and planning tasks**, carrying out sequences of actions or strategies, and making decisions. This field is closely linked to the autonomy of entities, and the associated technologies are used mainly by **intelligent agents, autonomous robots** and **autonomous vehicles**. It's a field that has to find complex solutions to complex problems whose context is strongly linked to the environment, and consequently to the actions to be taken in unknown multidimensional environments.

In **known environments** with available models, planning can be carried out outside any action, and **solutions can be found and evaluated before execution**.

However, in **unknown environments**, models must be adapted and adaptable, and **strategy must be dynamic and revised in real time**.

The aim of this domain is to manage intermediate states until the state declared as the final state is reached. To achieve this, we start with initial states, a description of desired goals and a description of all possible actions. We then need to build plans (this is the role of the agents) which ensure that, by starting from the initial states and using the possible actions, we arrive at the final state, and that the latter satisfies the defined goals.

6. Natural language

The definition of natural language as language understood and spoken by a human being is to be distinguished from formal languages and computer languages. In the context of artificial intelligence, the domain of natural language is **the understanding of a language by a machine and communication with humans** through it.

Of course, some languages are more complicated than others, the complexity of a language depending essentially on the **ambiguities it conveys** (see example below) and the **richness of the grammar** it uses to structure it.

If I say: "Paul tells John that he has a headache." - How many people are we dealing with? Some would say two, others three. Indeed, it's three: "Paul", "John" or "he". But who's got a headache? There's no way of knowing without precise knowledge of the environment and context in which the phrase is uttered. And a problem could arise if an autonomous machine were to treat the headache. It's conceivable that the machine might get the wrong person, and that the person chosen might be allergic to some of the drugs prescribed.

Natural language processing involves a number of tools from the world of linguistics, such as syntax, semantics and contextual analysis. In the context of artificial intelligence, we speak of automatic natural language processing (**ANLP**) or automatic language processing (**ALP**), **a field that straddles the border between linguistics and computer science**.

Automatic natural language processing is considered to be the **foundation of other areas of** artificial intelligence...

7. Machine learning

Machine Learning is a field of artificial intelligence that concerns the **design**, **analysis**, **development** and **implementation of methods** and **algorithms** enabling a machine **to learn**, **evolve** and **acquire the knowledge** needed to perform tasks or solve complex problems.

There are three types of learning:

- **Supervised learning**: this enables the development of predictive models based on input and output data. In other words, it takes into account previous results.

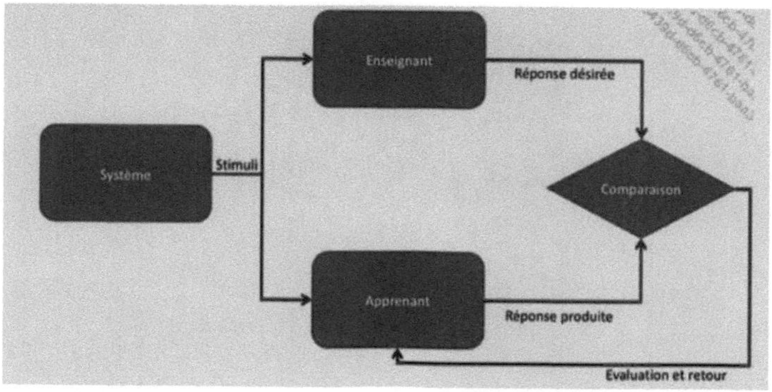

- **Unsupervised learning**: based on input data only. No expert is required; the system must find the more or less hidden structure of the input data on its own, and deduce explanations from it.

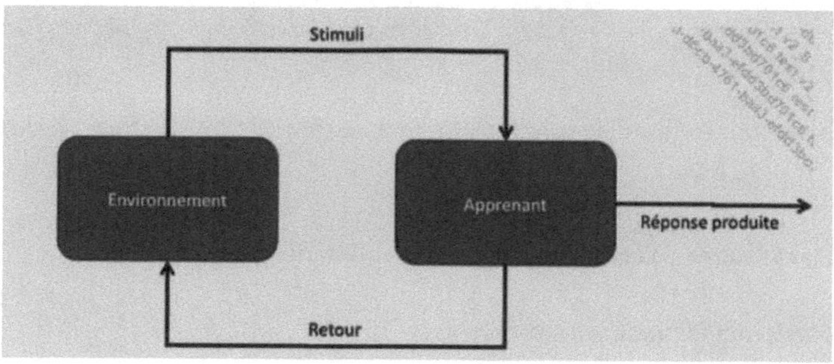

- **Reinforcement learning**: this refers to a class of machine learning problems whose aim is to learn, from experiments, what to do in different situations, so as to optimize a quantitative reward over time.

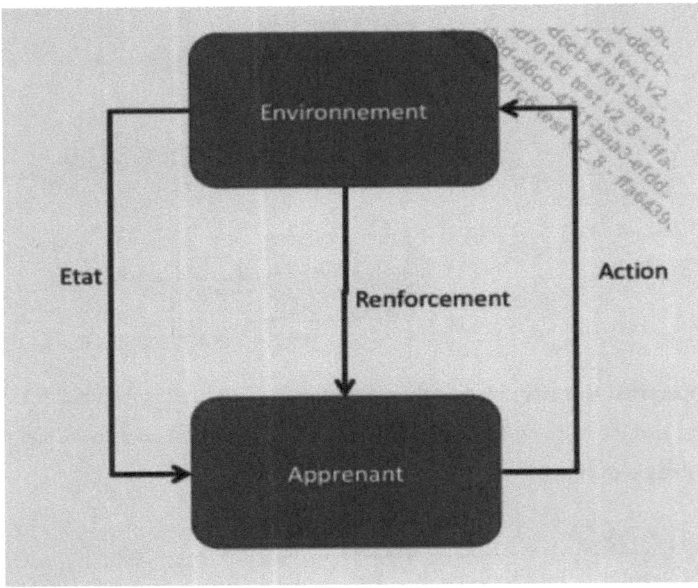

These three types of learning generate **different categories of algorithms**, which can be divided into three subtypes:

- **Classification** and **regression** for supervised learning.

- **Clustering** for unsupervised learning.

These algorithms are briefly described in the following sections. The aim is not to provide a complete description of the algorithms, but rather to provide a fairly general idea of how they work.

a. Classification

Classification is a category in the supervised mode of machine learning. **It is used to predict a category**. Data are used and classified in order to...

8. Automated reasoning

Automated reasoning is to be distinguished from the "reasoning" of expert systems, even if the latter can be considered as precursors. Indeed, expert systems give the impression of reasoning, because they know how to adapt to a situation and are able to reproduce the skills and reasoning of one or more experts in a particular field.

Automated reasoning, on the other hand, is a field of computer science dedicated to **understanding the different aspects of reasoning**, and to designing algorithms, methods and software that will enable machines to reason as a human would. It is usually regarded as a sub-field of artificial intelligence, where reasoning is intended to be automatic and should eventually enable machines to make autonomous decisions.

In order to understand the different aspects of reasoning, automatic reasoning, whether total or partial, draws on theoretical **computer science**, various **logics** (modal, formal, temporal, fuzzy), **mathematics** and even **philosophy**.

There isn't just one way of reasoning, but several that can be combined:

- **Reasoning by analogy**: we compare the assertion we want to evaluate with one or more assertions we've determined to be comparable, and whose result we know.
- **Reasoning by deduction**: starting from a general idea, principle or law, we draw a specific consequence.
- **Reasoning by induction**: we start from one or more specific facts to derive a principle, a law or a general idea. This is the opposite of reasoning by deduction.
- **Reasoning by abduction**: by observing one or more facts for which we know a possible and most likely cause, we take this cause as a hypothesis...

9. Decision-making

Decision-making **is the act of comparing several possibilities and making a choice** between several alternatives. This conscious, considered decision-making, which was the prerogative of humans, is now shared with machines.

Indeed, as we mentioned in the previous sections, the astronomical quantities of data generated by digital transformation, the emergence of intelligent machines, automated learning, predictive analysis, autonomous algorithms and intuitive interfaces will increase intelligent automation in all sectors. Already today, algorithms are able to detect what humans are incapable of seeing or imagining.

We're seeing an increase in decision-making support already integrated into many forms of work, from the most basic to the most cutting-edge. In many areas, **artificial intelligence tools have the potential to enhance human decision-making**, but also to **replace it entirely**. It is therefore important to regularly reassess the decision-making impact of the algorithms' preferences and assumptions.

Today, **machine decision-making** takes **three different forms**:

- **Assisted decision-making**: the human criticizes the decision that could be made by a machine. The results of the analysis and the decision(s) are provided to the human, who alone decides whether they are valid. As seen in automated learning, a reward system can be put in place.
- **Partial decision-making**: the human is assisted by the machine in making the decision. Intermediate decisions are made by the machine, with the human making the final decision. A set of alternative decisions can be provided by the machine, with the human then choosing one of them....

CHAPTER 6: ARTIFICIAL INTELLIGENCE (MACHINE LEARNING)

VLL ARTIFICIAL INTELLIGENCE (MACHINE LEARNING)

VI. 1.1 Definition

Machine learning is the technique of training a computer to identify patterns, make predictions and learn from past experience without explicit programming.

VI. 1.2 The difference between machine learning and artificial intelligence

Machine learning (or AA) is a sub-category of artificial intelligence (AI) that uses algorithms to identify patterns and make predictions in a set of data. This can be numbers, text or even images. Under ideal conditions, machine learning enables human beings to interpret data faster and more accurately than they would be able to do themselves.

VI. 1.3 How machine learning works

Artificial intelligence is a form of virtual intelligence that resembles that of a human being, created by humans in a machine. For machine learning, machines are programmed to reproduce specific cognitive functions that are natural to humans, such as perception, learning and problem-solving.

For a machine to think like a human, it must be trained to create its own predictive model. This model enables the machine to analyze data in order to become a "learning" machine. To start this process, you need to provide the computer with data and choose a learning model to tell the machine how to process the data.

A machine learning model can use data to perform three actions:

- describe an event ;
- predict an event;
- make suggestions for future action.

VI. 2.ROBOTICS, ROBOTS AND THINKING COMPUTERS

VI. 2.1 Robotics

VI. 2.1.1 Definition

Robotics is the science and technique of robotization, robot design and construction.

VI. 2.1.2 A brief history of robotics

Although the first **robots** were created in the USA in the 1960s, the word "robot" first appeared in Prague in the 1920s, in a play featuring humanoids. **Robot** comes from the Greek "robota", meaning chore. The first automata, however, are thought to have been produced much earlier, in the 18th century during the **Industrial Revolution.**

The word robotics comes from the English word robotics, and was first used in 1941 by the Russian science-fiction writer Isaac Asimov. In his short story Runaround, published in 1942, he presents the 3 main laws of **robotics**:

- A robot may not harm or expose a human being to danger.
- A robot must obey human orders.
- A robot must protect its own existence.

VI. 2.1.2 Example of robotics

- ✓ Robots in industrial assembly lines ;
- ✓ drones in the military ;
- ✓ NASA robots;
- ✓ operating room assistants in medicine;
- ✓ robot vacuum cleaners in the home;
- ✓ a voice assistant in computing...

VI. 2.1.3. fields of application for robotics

Robotics is used in a number of major fields:

- **Industry**: this is the preferred sector for robotics, where the machine can best help and replace man in the many tiring tasks. Assembly lines feature robots for welding, painting, etc.
- **The military**: autonomous vehicles are ideal for spy missions or for transporting

packs. They are often equipped with radar, infrared cameras, etc.

- **Healthcare**: robots are not autonomous in the medical field, but they do play a key role in assisting doctors and surgeons. This is known as assisted surgery.
- The **domestic environment**: for some years now, robots have been able to assist us in our homes and gardens, vacuuming, cleaning the pool, mowing the lawn...

VI. 2.1.4. Integrating robots into companies

Would you like to integrate a robot, i.e. a collaborative robot, into your organization? There are 3 main steps to follow:

- define a project team ;
- drawing up specifications;
- identifying the right partner.

In the case of a production site, there are 4 steps to be followed to ensure successful **integration:**

- project study ;
- control and programming of the collaborative robot ;
- operator training;
- setting up the maintenance contract.

VI. 2.1.5. The benefits of robotics

Intelligent robots are one of the **applications** of **artificial intelligence.** Autonomous or assisted, they can perform several tasks in a minimum of time, from simple to difficult and often tiring tasks. In industry, the historic sector of **robotics**, we know the advantages of its implementation:

- precision and speed ;
- reproducibility of tasks ;
- fewer errors ;
- shorter lead times;
- lower costs.

CHAPTER 7: ARTIFICIAL INTELLIGENCE (IA SEARCH ALGORITHMS)

VII. 1. Search algorithm

In computer science, a **search algorithm** is a type of algorithm which, for a given domain, a given problem and given criteria, returns as a result a set of solutions satisfying the problem.

Let's assume that the set of inputs is divisible into subsets, with respect to a given criterion, which may be, for example, an order relation. In general, such an algorithm checks a certain number of these inputs and returns one or more of the targeted inputs as output.

The set of all potential solutions in the domain is called the *search space.*

VII. 1.1. Classical search algorithms

On common data structures such as lists, tables or trees, there are *well-known* algorithms that can be easily implemented in the manner of a recipe. These algorithms exploit the properties of both the data structure and the domain.

A classic example is the dichotomous search, in which the search space is halved at each attempt, giving a logarithmic complexity (which is highly advantageous).

VII. 1.2 Complexity

These algorithms are at the heart of important questions in algorithmic complexity. They are also very important because of their wide range of applications.

VII. 1.3 Finding solutions to complex problems

For complex problems, the search for solutions is a matter for artificial intelligence.

- A brute-force search algorithm is one in which all inputs are checked one by one. This type of search can be effective if the solution space is of a reasonable size in relation to the power of the machine used to traverse it. It is therefore a method to be tried as a last resort if there is no other possibility.

- Heuristic searches are used when additional knowledge or properties make the search more efficient. For example, exploiting geometric symmetries to solve a puzzle can greatly reduce the *search space.* In the same way, a path search can be facilitated by even approximate knowledge of the direction in which the goal lies, or its distance.

VII. 1.4 Examples

- Sub-string search algorithm ;
- Pathfinding algorithm.

VII. 1.5 Other examples of the search algorithm

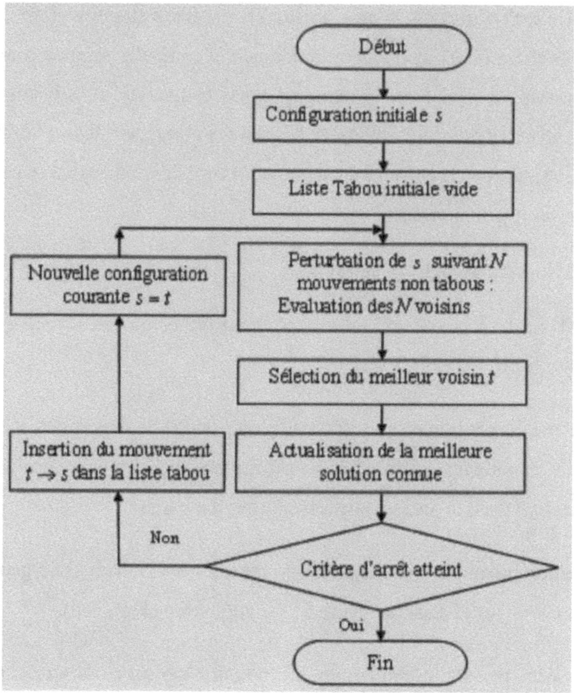

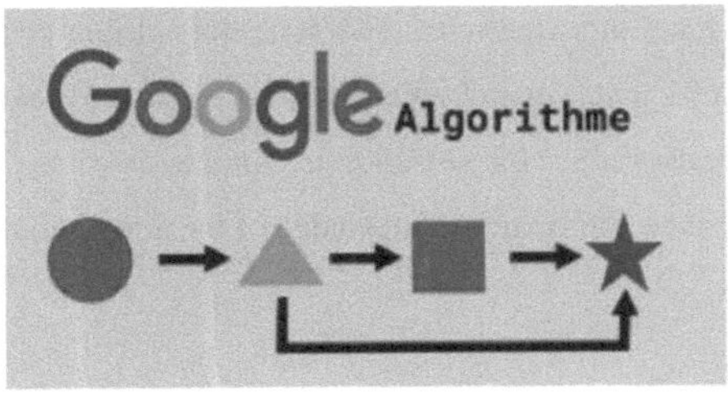

VII. 2.MINIMAX AND NEGAMAX ALGORITHMS

VII. 2.1 Minimax algorithms

VII. 2.1.1 Definition

The Minimax algorithm is an algorithm for solving strategy games between two players, such as chess or go. It draws on fundamental computer science concepts such as trees and recursion. It is also an example of a game-theoretic or artificial intelligence algorithm. It's an entry point for understanding how a computer "learns" or "thinks". It is likely to be of interest to a high-school student, as its application enables a certain number of games to be won with certainty.

VII. 2.1.2 Minimax algorithm sequence

The MINIMAX algorithm, designed by Von Neumann, aims to develop an optimal strategy for the MAX player.

At each turn, the MAX player chooses the move that will maximize his score, while minimizing his opponent's profits. These profits are evaluated in terms of the *static evaluation function* used to assess positions during the game.

For reasons of computation time and memory, the analysis is made for a game horizon of P, the number of moves ahead (the depth of the game tree examined).

As we have seen, the static evaluation of endgame positions is straightforward and precise: according to the rules of the game, it is necessary to assess whether it is a win, a loss or a tie. For intermediate positions, this function is imprecise, due to the more or less subjective criteria used for evaluation. The lack of accuracy of the static evaluation function is compensated for by the rigorous analysis of the consequences of each move made by two players.

The algorithm performs an evaluation of the current position, represented by the root of the game tree, starting from the terminal nodes. For this purpose, the set of nodes in the game tree is divided into two classes: MAX nodes for the levels at which this player will make a move, and MIN nodes for the MIN player's decision levels.

Example. Consider that during a game of *Tic Tac Toe* you have reached the position shown in the root of the tree in figure 3.4.2. We can see that the first level is colored yellow, so it's player ***X***'s (the MAX player) turn to play.

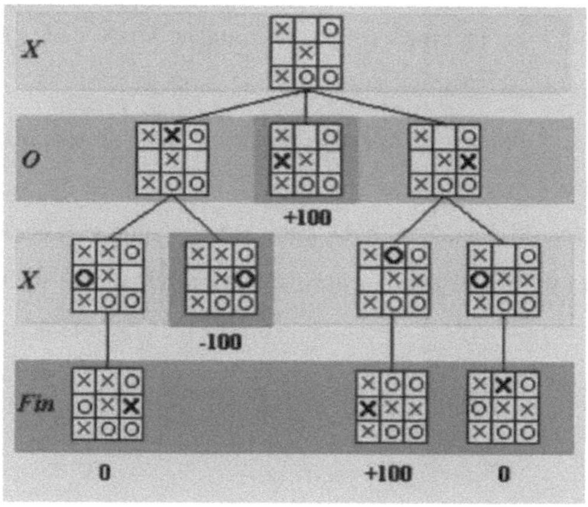

The decision levels for the MIN player are colored blue, and the terminal positions are shown in green, with the values of the static devaluation function written below.

The game tree corresponding to this position is shown in figure 3.4.3. MAX and MIN nodes are represented by triangles. MIN nodes are distinguished from MAX nodes by the position of the triangle and, in general, are not colored. But to keep an easy correspondence with the situation in figure 3.4.2, we've colored the nodes with the same colors as the players' decision levels.

Under the terminal nodes (either MIN or MAX, but all colored green) we've marked the value of the static evaluation function (+100 for a MAX win, 0 for a draw, and -100 for a MIN win).

The MINIMAX algorithm associates a value with the root, according to which the MAX player will choose his move. An algorithm for the agent implementing the MAX player will include the following phases:

- Building the game tree for *P* levels
- Visit the game tree *level by level,* working up from the terminal nodes to the root:
  - o if the current node *p* represents a terminal position, it is assigned the value of the static devaluation function, f(*p*)
  - o if it is an intermediate position and a MIN node, it is assigned the smallest of the values associated with its children
  - o if it is an intermediate position and a MAX node, it is assigned the maximum value associated with its children.
- When we've succeeded in associating a value with the root (called the *MiniMax* value*),* we choose the move that leads to the son with this maximum value. If there are several threads with the same value, then one is chosen at random (or the one that leads to victory, or the one that leads to a final situation in the fewest moves, or another criterion depending on the specifics of the game).

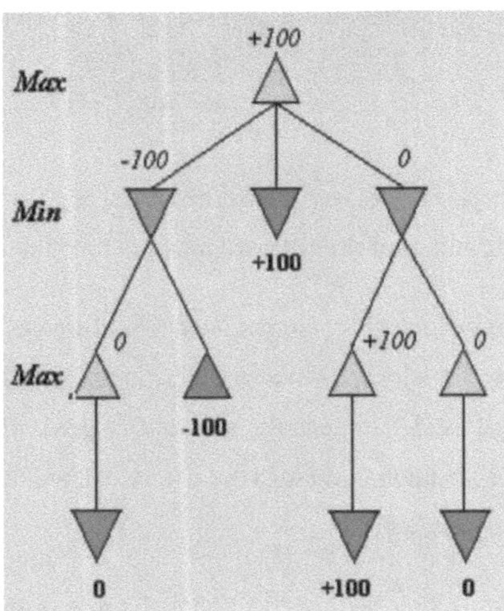

Example. Figure 3.4.3 shows the process of associating values to the intermediate nodes, marked in *italics.* The *MiniMax* value obtained (+100) is the best possible value from the position considered, and in this case brings victory in one move for the MAX player, if he heads for the son located in the middle of the figure. If he chooses to go for the son on the left, which has an associated value of -100, he will lose the game, if the opponent plays optimally. If he goes for the wire with the associated value 0, he'll get a zero result.

The *MiniMax* value determined cannot guarantee victory for the MAX player, but will always lead him to the best possible situation for the given position.

Example. The match game. At the start of the game, there are a few matches on a table. Each player in turn can choose to take 1, 2 or 3 matches at a time. The player who takes the last match loses. The MINIMAX tree for the situation with 5 matches on the table and the MAX agent's turn is shown in figure 3.4.4, where the triangles show the numbers of matches on the table before the move.

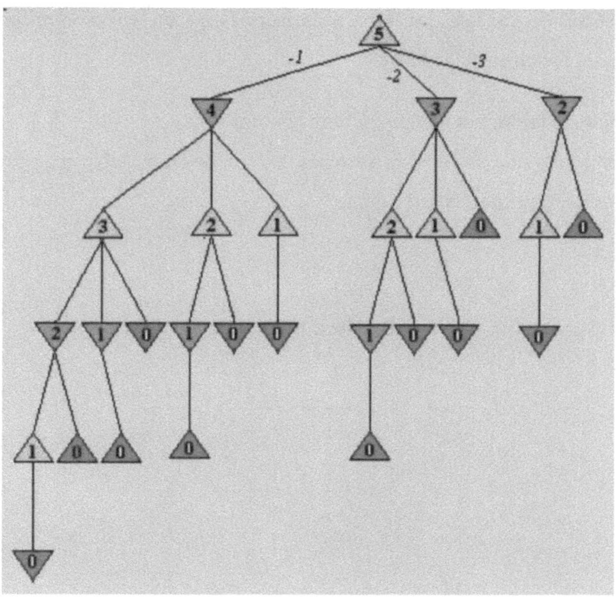

The operators that model the moves are -1, -2, -3 (the number of matches that are taken by the agent) and they are always applied in this order, from left to right in the game tree shown. For the first three arcs starting from the initial position, we've shown the number of matches removed, but to simplify the drawing we haven't shown it on the arcs of the other levels. The static evaluation function assigns the value +100 to a successful end position for the MAX agent, and -100 to a losing position.

If we determine the *MiniMax* value for the situation with 5 matches on the table and the MAX player's turn, we'll find -100, so the MAX player will lose the game if the MIN player plays logically. We can see that the values associated with all the MIN nodes succeeding the root are equal to -100, so whatever operator the MAX agent applies (the move), we'll arrive at a winning position for the MIN player.

In fact, if the MAX agent withdraws 1 match, the MIN agent in turn withdraws 3, if MAX withdraws 2, MIN also withdraws 2, and if MAX withdraws 3, MIN will withdraw 1. In all these situations, MAX will find 1 match on the table, which it will be forced to take, so it will lose the game.

Questions. Consider the leftmost direct successor of the root, which corresponds to a position with 4 matches on the table.

1) What are the values associated with his sons?

2) What is the n-value (n<5) of the matches that can be on the table and, if it' s the MAX player' s turn, can he win the game?

Answer

The MINIMAX algorithm can be described by the following pseudo code.

```
fonction MINIMAX( p) est
    maxime = -MAX_VAL
    pour *) chacune fils = successeur(p) faire
        val_fils = ValeurMINI(fils)
        si val_fils > maxime alors
            maxime = val_fils
            coup = fils
    fin pour
    retourner coup
Fin
```

```
fonction ValeurMINI ( n ) est
    si  Feuille( n )= vrai alors
        retourner f(n)
    sinon
        v_min = MAX_VAL
        pour *) chacune fils = successeur(p) faire
            v_fils = ValeurMAX(fils)
            v_min = min (v_min, v_fils)
        fin pour
    fin si
    retourner v_min
Fin
```

```
fonction ValeurMAX ( n ) est
    si  Feuille( n )= vrai alors
        retourner f(n)
    sinon
        v_max = -MAX_VAL
        pour *) chacune fils = successeur(p) faire
            v_fils = ValeurMINI(fils)
            v_max= max(v_max,v_fils)
        fin pour
    fin si
    retourner v_max
Fin
```

The functions max(x,y) and min(x,y) return the largest / smallest value of the set {x , y}. The function Leaf(n) returns **true** if node n is a terminal node (end of game or terminal node when searching a game tree with limited depth P).

The function MINIMAX calls the function ValueMINI(threads) for all threads of the root *p* (the initial position), because all threads of the root are MINI nodes. Indirect recursion: theMINI(n)value function calls theMAX(child) value function, which in turn calls theMINI(child) value function, thus ensuring !alternating MINI - MAX processing in !exploring the game tree.

Question : What type of exploration in the game tree performs the MINIMAX algorithm shown?

Answer

Analysis of the MINIMAX algorithm

Complete - yes, if !game tree is finite

Optimal - yes, if the MAX player has an opponent who plays optimally

Time complexity - $\boldsymbol{O}(b^{(P})$)

Complexity in place - for a deep exploration of the game tree first ***O(bP)***

It should be pointed out that for complex games, the exact solution cannot be found in a reasonable amount of time. For example, the game of chess has a branching factor b=35 and for common games *P=100*, so we get a number of treatments of the order of 35^{100}, which is a giant number (for comparison, the number of atoms in the universe is of the order of $10^{100)}$. We need to find more practical strategies.

VII. 2.2. The Negamax algorithm

VII.2.2.1 Definition

The Negamax algorithm is a powerful technique used to solve problems in zero-sum games.

Zero-sum games are those where one player's gain is exactly the other's loss. The objective of the Negamax algorithm is to optimize and simplify Minimax in such contexts. The underlying principle of Negamax is that it uses the symmetry of zero-sum games to express position values in opposite terms, rather than using the Min and Max functions separately.

VII.2.2.2. How Negamax works

Negamax works recursively by evaluating possible moves and assigning a negative score to the opponent for each move. This negation simplifies calculations, as it allows us to work with a single evaluation function, assuming that the current player tries to maximize his score while the opponent minimizes it.

VII.2.2.3. Algorithm pseudocode

The Negamax pseudopode is generally presented as follows:

```
function negamax(node, depth, color):
    if node is a terminal state or depth = 0:
        return color * evaluate(node)

    bestValue = -infinite
    for each child in node:
        value = -negamax(child, depth - 1, -color)
        bestValue = max(bestValue, value)
    return bestValue
```

VII.3. STRENGTHS AND WEAKNESSES OF THE MINIMAX OR NEGAMAX SEARCH ALGORITHM

VII.3.1. Strength of the Minimax or Negamax search algorithm

It ensures that the player makes the best possible move, taking into account all possible outcomes. For example, the tic-tac-toe mini max algorithm evaluates all possible moves and chooses the one that leads to victory or blocks the opponent's potential victory. The algorithm's logic is easy to understand and implement.

VII.3.2. Weaknesses of Minimax or Negamax search algorithms

Firstly, they are based on the assumption that the game is fully observable, deterministic and has perfect information.

Secondly, their effectiveness is highly dependent on the complexity of the game and the branching factor of the game tree.

CHAPTER 8: PRACTICE

BIBLIOGRAPHY

❖ **Books**

- Guide en appui au Programme Educatif du Domaine d'Apprentissage des Sciences, 2021 edition.
- **Ashrafian Hutan, Darzi Ara, Athanasiou Thanos**: A novel modi-fication of the Turing test for artificial intelligence and robotics in healthcare. Int J. Med Robot, 2015.
- **CAPTCHA**, a fully automatic public Turing test designed to distinguish humans from computers.
- **Chabot, Pascal**. Chatbot the robot. Paris: PUF, 2015.
- **Chabot, Pascal**. What on earth are chatbots for? Challenges, 1erFebruary 2017.
- **Turing, Alan and Girard, Jean-Yves**. Computers and Intelligence: The Turing Machine. Éditions du Seuil, 1995.
- **Weizenbaum, Joseph.** ELIZA - A Computer Program For the Study of Natural Language Communication Between Man And Machine. Communications of the ACM, January 1966.

❖ **Websites :**

- www.inmac-wstore.com
- www.phpeasydata.com
- www.codyx.org
- www.saveho.com,
- www.larousse.fr

Kolibri 360 GmbH
Ferdinand-Jühlke-Straße 7
99095 Erfurt, Deutschland
produktsicherheit@kolibri360.de

Druck:
CPI Druckdienstleistungen GmbH
im Auftrag der
Kolibri 360 GmbH
Ferdinand-Jühlke-Str. 7
99095 Erfurt